Energetic Hypnosis

Tutorial: Professional Trance States

by

Dr. Claus Wunderlich

ISBN 9798692660015

Independently published
Dr. Claus Wunderlich, Munich, Germany

Author: Dr. Claus Wunderlich

Cover: Tino Petzold

Foreword to the English Edition

The tremendous and surprising success of the original German edition of this book resulted in numerous requests to make the fascinating content available to international readers, too.

Thus, it was imperative to offer an English translation. As far as I know, the ideas that will be presented in this book have not been spread in English language till now. This afforded to take as much care in the translation as possible.

In particular, the transcribed hypnosis session of Chapter 12 was actually done in German language, of course. It was mandatory to meet the challenge that all the key aspects and subtleties are kept.

I counterchecked the result and, hence, I am very pleased and excited to be able to approve that I am completely satisfied with the pages that you hold in your hands.

I am convinced that you we will enjoy this book as much as the readers of the German edition did.

Dr. Claus Wunderlich
Munich, Germany
August 2020

Table of Contents

Exercises

1. Introduction

Energetic-Hypnosis is the result of many years of experience in the field of personal development. Thus, many different traditional approaches have been integrated and important advances could be achieved.

The holistic approach of Energetic-Hypnosis demands not only to resolve the current topic or problem but to start extensive energetic processes whitin the client's subconscious mind in order to transform and enrich his complete personality. This is also true regarding self-hypnosis.

In the course of this book you will learn all the basics of Energetic-Hypnosis. This will be supported by exercises, which will allow you to make your own experiences right away. Thus, you will become more and more familiar with the infinite opportunities of your subconscious.

Tying this altogether, you will be optimally prepared for the central climax of this book: a commented transcript of an Energetic-Hypnosis-Session. It is highly recommended to work through it first without reading the comments. This offers you the chance to optimally embed all the learnings in your mind and subsequently be able to use them in a professional way. For the sake of convenience, the ongoings of the session are printed on the left half of each page while the explanations are on the right. Thus, it is possible to easily cover them and expose them step by step if desired. This also stresses the interactive character of this book, which is designed more in the way of an exercise book than a text book and incorporates the ideas of accelerated learnings.

In the epilogue I offer you a story that will enrich your subconscious mind in a very subtle and effective manner. It is the bright final of a hopefully fascinating adventure that this lecture shall offer to you. This is my honest wish.

What are the differences and what are the similarities of Energetic-Hypnosis compared to other well-known and effective approaches? In common with the Autogenic Trainig by Schultz and the Progressive Muscle-Relaxation by Jacobson is the very extreme physical relaxation and the intense perception of all areas of the own body. But Energetic-Hypnosis results in an even deeper physical resting state and it also aims at a complete mental liberation. In that sense similar to certain meditations, it offers on the one hand more comfortable body positions and also does not want to end in an emptiness of the mind, which shall result in some sort of enlightenment. Contrary to that, Energetic-Hypnosis wants to release the inherent creative powers, which are often obstructed by subconscious incrustations. Additionally, actual questions and topics are precisely addressed.

This emphasis and determination on achieving goals is mainly due to the proposals of Neuro-Linguistic Programming. Hence, it is not surprising that some of its methods and formats have been incorporated. However without adopting its often quite rigid theoretical guidelines.

Very close are of course the relations to the classical hypnotic procedures, though Energetic-Hypnosis reaches beyond in many regards. The ancient antagonism between Ericksonians on the one side and the authoritarian school on the other is overcome in a way that the most successful elements of both are combined and incorporated.

And the very important aspect of activating the individual energetic vitality on a subconscious level is added. This reaches back to the founders of modern psychology, like Freud and Jung, which gave us the idea of the subconscious[1] and its almost infinite possibilities, either good or bad.

Hypnosis itself may not be confused with narcosis. A person is neither without will in hypnosis or completely at somebody else's mercy nor totally separated from his surrounding.[2] Though it is true that in very deep trance states the environment fades almost completely, the subconscious itself is even more alert and will suspend the hypnotic state whenever something happens that contradicts the own values, goals or interests. Modern science has proven that the brain is highly active in hypnosis but the activity takes place in completely different areas than in the waking state.

Don't be too surprised if you get the impression that you can only partly or fuzzily remember what you have read in this book. This is intended and an excellent sign because it proves that you have received the information on a subconscious level, which will allow the complete effect to optimally develop. Like a dream that you just remembered and now cannot grasp any more. Yet, the memory is still completely stored and the effect even increases if the conscious mind is no longer able to intervene or disturb with its critical perspective.

I shall present the important and central concepts of hypnosis but avoid lengthy historical and theoretical discussions because one of the prime ideas of this book is to offer you the chance to learn a lot of new and unexpected

----

1   Subconscious and unconscious are, in this sense, mainly synonyms and, thus, only the first one will be used throughout this book.

2   Recently, there are hints that patients in narcosis perceive everything that happens around them, too. Especially, using hypnosis afterwards revealed that they had stored word-by-word what was spoken by the staff. The implications are quite worrying.

aspects about yourself. I highly recommend to do the exercises thoroughly and with care. Not only because they are lots of fun but also to get the most out of this book. Much more than by only reading and skipping them. Of course this is also an option and entirely up to you. Preferable you should have pen and paper right at hand. So, let's start with a little thrilling exercise right away.

Exercise: The Bear

Now there are three short and quite similar stories about a bear. Decide intuitively which is your favourite. Later in the book, you will get some very interesting remarks on that topic. This may also offer you some new ideas about the way your mind operates.

Story 1

Once upon a time, there was a huge bear with a shining dark brown fur and bright black eyes. He lived in a forest full of shadows. Every day, late in the afternoon, he went to visit a tiny clearing which at that time was always flooded with sunshine that made it glow in a very unique red-golden light. The bear looked around because there were many interesting things to behold. Lots of beautiful flowers with different blossoms in every colour, more intense than at any other time of the day or any other location. And he watched the bees and the butterflies with their red and yellow and blue wings. He loved to look around and he enjoyed the beauty of this place till the dawning made the light fade more and more. As soon as the darkness of the night had arrived, he went home and the sparks of hundreds of fireflies and thousands of shining stars showed him the way. Back in his dark cave, he laid himself down, closed his eyes and started to dream vividly.

Story 2

Once upon a time, there was a huge bear living deep in the woods. Every day, late in the afternoon, he used to follow the twittering birds to his favourite location in the forest, a silent meadow. This was the place, where he could listen to the sound of the little river that ran in the distance, and the singing of the birds. Some of them made whistling sounds while others sang wonderful melodies. From time to time a buzzing bee came across and when the noise of the wind became more intense, he knew that the evening has come and now a different kind of orchestra would accompany his way back to his cavern: the cries of the owls and the choirs of nightingales. Tired he laid himself down to rest, grumbling and yawning.

Story 3

Once upon a time, there was a huge bear living in a wood full of trees. He had a cosy fur and tender eyes. Every afternoon he enjoyed the mild temperature at his favourite location, a comfortable meadow that was surrounded by brushwood. He laid on the soft grass and inhaled the smell of the flowers around him. When the warming rays of the sun faded and a cooling breeze touched him, he wandered back to his cave and relaxed a little bit before he placed his heavy head on his cushion and covered his big body with a thick blanket. Soon he fell asleep.

1. Which of the stories did you like best?

O Story 1   O Story 2   O Story 3

2. Which of the three stories did you like least?

O Story 1   O Story 2   O Story 3

3. What kinds of differences between the stories did you notice?

____

____

____

____

____

____

____

____

Let me add some notes about the three different kinds of people that usually visit a coach or a therapist.

1. Clients

Persons with a real request for support and a substantial motivation to change and develop their personality, behaviour and life. They usually posses a clear-cut idea which kind of assistance they desire and what goal they want to reach with the therapy.

2. Visitors

That kind of people is most of the times sent, or at least motivated, by somebody else to seek professional support. Mainly by mates, parents, superiors, doctors or even state authorities. This already gives a hint that the urge to change anything within their life or behaviour is usually rather limited. Yet, meeting them can be funny and joyous most of the times for both the visitor and the coach. But it won't have any effect. It is not only the missing motivation to give up beloved habits, it is also the more fundamental question whether the therapists should even aim at any change because obviously this is not the declared interest of the person in front of them. At least not at this moment in time.

3. Complainers

The really problematic individuals are those with a determined intention to throw their frustrations and emotional disappointments at somebody else. Apparently they have a defined issue but actually they do not have the slightest interest in dealing with it in a constructive manner. Often this shows up immediately because they tend to reject any offers of support or change by using all sorts of good reasons that allegedly prevent exactly these possibilities. Instead, they continue with an endless stream of complaints about all imaginable aspects of life and mankind. The effect may not be underrated. Most of the times, someone like that feels much better after an hour of wailing and blaming. Of course not for long, for nothing has really changed. But the other person often is left behind feeling like an empty hull. Thus, these complainers are sometimes even called 'emotional vampires'. It is extremely important for the sake of the own well-being to protect oneself emotionally against these persons without any guilty conscience. You are not able to achieve anything anyway.

As a corollary an interesting question arises, whether these three categories also apply to the buyers and readers of books like the one in front of you. And to which category oneself belongs to. The gain from reading such literature might heavily depend on the answer.

2. Emotions

One can hardly overestimate the importance of emotions when dealing with the topic of self development. Especially facing the fact that many human are not able to access their feelings to an extent that would be useful or even possible. It is important to note the distinction between the generalized descriptions of certain emotions (like 'fear', 'anger', 'joy') and the physiological sensations they are based on.

These descriptions merely circumscribe a bunch of perceptions inside the body that got labelled that way by the respective person. For example 'anger': remember a situation that made you feel really angry. And now guide your attention to all the different sensations in your body. Some people may feel a pulsation in the belly, heavy breathing, rapid heartbeat, a clenching of a fist, some pressure in the head, warmth in the face and a tightening of the muscles in the legs. Others might experience a completely different combination of physical reactions that are associated with the word 'anger'.

What is the reason for these differences? One very plausible theory states that, as a child, you had at some point certain physical sensations without already possessing any name for them. In this pre-verbal phase somebody, usually a close relative, told you something like, "You are angry!". From this moment on, this specific mix of body sensations was labelled as anger.

This demonstrates that the word 'anger' does not necessarily possess the identical meaning to everybody. It depends mainly on the special combination of physiological perceptions that a person experienced when the name was given and accepted. Of course, this is not eternally hardwired and certain adaptations can and will occur in the further development of the individual. Especially through feedback by family members and close friends. And it is obvious that most people do have quite similar associations connected with the various emotional labels. This is of course an effect of cultural influences, too. But think for a moment of more complex feelings, like 'love' for example, then you might get an idea of the broadness of the variety of emotional meanings that different individuals attach to it.

A fascinating aspect is the rapid detachment of the label from its physiological foundation. This means that most persons are no longer aware of what is happening in their body. Asked, what is felt in an emotionally intense situation, the answer you get is most of the times one of the labels which we were talking about. Insisting on more information about the precise physical sensations that the individual experienced in that situation, will often result in surprise and confusion and not knowing what the question is all about. Because the answer has already been given, hasn't it? It affords some amount of time and carefulness to reach all the basic experiences of the emotion. The word 'feeling' has its linguistic origin in a kinaesthetic occurrence.

Association vs. Dissociation

To experience one's own feelings straight is called being associated with them and with oneself. The opposite is dissociation. This describes a state of being separated from one's feelings, like watching yourself from the outside.

Both is neither good nor bad, depending on the context. Especially regarding unpleasant feelings, it can be very helpful and positive to be able to dissociate from them. At least as long as direct perception does not make any sense for solving a problem. Additionally, it is usually easier and more productive to reflect intellectually about an event in a dissociated state of mind. On the other side, it seems quite useful to be associated with oneself in pleasant situations. Certainly you can imagine some.

Besides the fact that many people posses an impressive talent to dissociate themselves from pleasant feelings but experience bad feelings fully associated, there is the phenomenon that most people nowadays are alienated from their emotions altogether.[3] You can recognize this quite easily because they avoid to speak of themselves in terms of first person singular.

The mildest form of getting around the 'I' is to use a fuzzy 'We'. This at least includes the speaker theoretically. More detached and somewhat bizarre seems the usage of second person singular, i.e. 'You', when speaking about one's own experiences. But the most common version is the word 'one'. Pay attention, how many people that one meets every day have eliminated the little phrase 'I' almost completely from their vocabulary and talk about themselves permanently in third person. I leave to you the decision whether they also think and feel about themselves in the same way.

____

3 Which of these two alternatives is the less desirable, is open to discussion.

Exercise: Emotions

1. Put yourself successively into the following emotional states.[4] Do this fully associated. For example, by vividly remembering an appropriate event. Note extensively every sensation from your head down to your feet. Be as precise as possible. Notice the location and intensity of your perceptions. Furthermore, watch if something is moving or pulsing.

Fear:

____

____

____

Sadness:

____

____

____

Anger:

____

____

____

---

4 These are the basic emotions that Paul Ekman discovered in different cultures around the world in his seminal studies. Of course, the English language possesses many more and much more complex emotional descriptions.

Joy:

____

____

____

Surprise:

____

____

____

Disgust:

____

____

____

2. Add another emotion that are important in your life and repeat the exercise with it.

Other Emotion:

____

____

____

3. Place yourself in front of a mirror and associate yourself again with the various emotional states. Watch your facial expressions. If you like, you can also note what strikes you.

---

4. Take this exercise as a proposition to do this every day whenever you experience a situations with intense feelings. Take a moment to perceive all the sensations in your body. Maybe you will get some surprises. Anyway, our little exercise did best prepare you for it.

Beyond the already described semantic removal of the emotional label from its physiological meaning exists an even more severe mechanism that inhibits the individual access to one's own feelings. An effect that is responsible for a broad spectrum of problems. Very often at an age when they were most susceptible human beings are prohibited either to express their feelings or even to experience them at all. While usually the first tends to become the second sooner or later anyway.

Unnecessary to mention that none of the feelings that can be affected, are either good or bad, wrong or right, justified or not. These categories are simply inadequate. Feelings exist. Periood! Everything else is a kind of judgement that is quite inappropriate. Of course, there are events that are misinterpreted and, thus, might cause reactions that might seem strange or out of place. But that is not the same like regarding an emotional effect as wrong.
Obviously, this does not excuse in any way every kind of behaviour that is displayed under intense emotions. This is absolutely due to judgements and evaluations. But the mere experiencing and verbal expressing of feelings should be everybody's basic right.

However, there are situations when one person is not able to cope with emotions of another because they are embarrassing, unpleasant or annoying. Or it might be the case that they are rated immoral. The most often affected emotions should be anger, sadness, pain and fear, but also pleasure and joy.

If the person is in some way dependent on the others that dislike certain emotional expressions, they posses different options to show their contempt and eventually cause the suppression of the unwanted feelings. This can be done by cold verbal rejection, by means of withdrawal of love and attention, through isolation, threatening or even violence.[5]

Unfortunately, the emotions are only suppressed but not eliminated. Either they will break through ferociously from time to time, often without any real cause. Or they may find different ways or different targets instead. And maybe they will turn into other emotional shapes. One of the not forbidden alternatives that are allowed to be experienced and expressed.

Excursus: Virginia Satir

Virginia Satir, the pioneer in family therapy, developed the concept that human beings tend to react in one of four ways when exposed to emotional pressure. This is especially true in situations that afford to hide certain feelings from oneself or others.

1.   Blaming: noisy, accusing, dominant, aggressive, slagging off everyone and everything – to disguise the feeling of being worthless and hurt.

2.   Placating: excusing, silent, submissive, justifying, appeasing, taking every blame – to not have to feel the fear of being completely lost without the other.

3.   Computing: extremely rational, logical, objective, intellectual – living the idea of not feeling any pain as long as one does not feel anything at all.

4.   Distracting: basically a rapid alternation of the other three patterns, lengthy explanations with hardly any substance – to avoid any feeling as quick as possible in order to let nobody realise how disliked and lost one feels.

---

5   In this context, a very import issue deals with so-called 'selfishness'. Nowadays, the pursuit of one's own interests is often officially declared as negative and, from various sides, one is taught from an early age on that it is shameful, evil, antisocial, morally reprehensible, etc. to think of oneself and one's own needs. Of course, such judgments are merely subjective opinions. For example, Ayn Rand, the great philosopher of the 20th Century, expressed an ethically completely contrary and highly positive view on human selfishness. Much more interesting, yet, is the fact that such stigmatisation of selfish thoughts and actions is usually conveyed with purely selfish motivations. After all, who has been successfully manipulated to only take care of the declared weal and woe of others is a subservient pawn to the interests of the other. Important for our concerns is, primarily, the inherent contradiction of demonising 'selfishness' for selfish motives, which is hardly recognisable for the victim of such double standards and brainwashing. Such pragmatic paradoxes, called 'double binds' by Paul Watzlawick, possess substantial pathogenic power.

Recognizing and correctly assigning these categories offers important hints about what is really going on within a person and to what extent the negation of feelings is an issue.

Exercise: Satir

Think of different individuals who you know quite well. Which of the four patterns do they usually reveal faced with emotional stress?

It should now have become obvious that in many cases affective energies are distracted massively towards destructive pathways. The very suppression of emotions itself affords massive effort which inevitably happens subconsciously. As a consequence, all the people close to that person are affected, especially because the emotions which one denies oneself are also forbidden for others and will be prosecuted, hence. This gives one a slight idea of the vast consequences that this effect may cause. With no doubt, this also means a giant tragedy to the person concerned because there won't be any chance for substantial joy in live or even a happy existence if the access to the most basic feelings is not only blocked but has to be actively suppressed all the time.

For that reason, it is the central concern of Energetic-Hypnosis to offer the client the explicit allowance of living his own feelings and getting complete access. Following Virginia Satir's advice that everybody shall be free to speak about what is really felt and thought, instead of acting the way it is expected to, and that every person shall be free to articulate their real feelings instead of pretending something else.

3. Kinesiology and the O-Ring-Test

Kinesiology comprises a number of methods and techniques which are based on the idea that the intensity of muscular strength offers information about the emotional state of a person.

If a person experiences stress, for example because she is telling a lie, this results in a significant lessening of muscular tension which in turn can be detected quite easily. Usually this is done either by measuring the strength of the arm or the index finger and thumb.[6] This last method is known as O-Ring-Test (or Omura-Ring-Test).

These tests are quite common in coaching and therapy whenever it is important to get information about the emotions or motivations that a client is not aware of. They can even be helpful in exploring repressed traumas that stem from the earliest childhood. Psychoanalysis and Transactional Analysis both offer the notion that events in that phase of life have fundamental consequences for the whole existence of an individual.

For illustrative purposes, you may think for a moment of the effect that your current mood has on your personal strength.

Every experiencing or remembering of events that are associated with negative feelings leads to an emotional state which inevitably weakens the muscular tension of a person. Of significant importance is also the reaction of other people. This generates not only mental but also physiological effects. The phenomenon of dependence on the visible reactions of other people is deeply grounded and even the sight of a sketched face may have a measurable effect on a person, depending on whether the face is smiling or frowning.

Exercise: Arm-Test

For this exercise you need a partner.

First: draw the two graphs on a sheet of paper each:

---

6   Or, in a more sophisticated way, by the use of a polygraph.

1. Keep the two drawings covered. Ask your partner to hold one of his arms stretched horizontally and as tight as possible.

Now show the picture with the smiling face and try to pull down his arm. You should not be very successful (at least if you are not much stronger). Take this picture away and show the other one with the frowning face instead. Try again to pull down your partner's arm. It is highly probable that you will experience much less resistance this time. Remember that the only difference is the view of a sketch of a laughing vs. a frowning face.

2. Exchange your roles and repeat the exercise in order to get the experience of the other position yourself.

One of the most elegant methods is the so-called O-Ring-Test. It was devised by the New York physician Dr. Yoshiaki Omura. The procedure demands that the client forms an 'O' with his thumb and index finger and presses them together as tight as he is able to. The coach evaluates the emotional state of the client by trying to pull them apart. As long as the coach is not substantially stronger, he will not have much success in doing so. But as soon as the client experiences emotional pressure, his strength diminishes noticeable and the two fingers should be separable to some extent with little force.

Because the reactions may vary from person to person, it is essential to calibrate. This can be achieved by asking some trivial questions, like the client's name or the current date. Each question is to be answered with, "Yes!", regardless whether that was correct. After two or three questions that are answered truthfully, a question is added, which is not correctly answered with, "Yes!". Even a lie that unimportant will cause stress and effect the tension of the muscles. Now a difference should be detectable in the power that keeps thumb and index finger pressed together.

As an example, you may ask a client with the name Mary on a Thursday whether she is called 'Mary' and if today is 'Thursday'. Next ask her, "Is your name Britney?" and, "Today is Saturday, right?" During the clients answer, the coach tries to separate the clients fingers each time. There should be a marked difference between correct and incorrect answers.

From now on, the whole range of possible applications is available to discover emotional pressure. One interesting aspect is the opportunity to precisely find the age, at which an imprinting event took place. Within the context of interpersonal work in hypnosis, the various kinesiological tests are the prime choice in discovering energetic problems and for evaluating whether an intervention was successful in modifying the emotional state of a client.

Exercise: O-Ring-Test

For this exercise you need a partner.

1. Ask your partner to form an 'O' with the thumb and the index finger of one of his hands and to press them together tightly. Now try if you are able to separate them.

Ask your partner now to answer each question with a "Yes!", regardless whether this is the correct answer or not. Each time try to pry his fingers.

Now start with some questions that are correctly answered with a "Yes!" (e.g. name, day, age). Are you able to separate your partner's fingers?

Next ask some questions that are not correctly answered with a "Yes!". Because your partner will answer, "Yes!" in these cases as well, you should notice that it has become much more easy to separate the two fingers. To what extent are you able to separate the fingers?

2. Exchange the roles and repeat the exercise in order to get the experience of the other position yourself.

4. Representational Systems

The term 'representational system' describes each of the five senses that human beings use to perceive their environment:

1.   Visual

2.   Auditory

3.   Kinaesthetic (Body Feelings)

4.   Olfactory (Smell)

5.   Gustatory (Taste)

Other well-known expressions to describe the representational systems are modalities, sensory modalities or senses.

The precise classification is to some extent open to discussion. Especially the feeling of temperature, the experience of physical pain or the sensations inside the body are sometimes regarded as independent senses beside 'Kinaesthetic'. For the sake of simplicity, we will not further pursue these subtleties because they are neither necessary nor helpful.

Today it is scientifically proven that there are more than our familiar five senses, for example the one for balance. Further more, there are some that are outside our conscious awareness, like the sensory receptors for the blood pressure inside the throat or the ones in the nose that react on pheromones.

Whether there is something like a '6th sense' for extrasensory perception, is an interesting question. The astounding intuition that some people are able to demonstrate sometimes almost seems like telepathy.

A surprising discovery is the fact that most people have a distinct preference for one of the representational systems, not only regarding the outside world but also with respect to their internal mental processes. Usually it is one of the three modalities Visual, Auditory or Kinaesthetic (abbreviated: VAK).[7] Of course, in most cases all senses are in use, yet, the emphasis differs quite impressively amongst individuals and one is usually significantly preferred.

Is it possible to recognize from the outside which sense is a persons primary one? Indeed there are signals that indicate that preference. First, the kind of

---

7 Once I met a guy whose primary representational system obviously was the gustatory one. He used an impressive amount of words that were accompanied with eating and drinking. And most of his conversations centred around these topics. Unnecessary to mention that this preference was reflected in his weight.

verbal expressions somebody uses. The way of thinking will inevitably be reflected in somebody's utterances. Thus, mainly words, in particular the verbs, of the primary representational system will be used to communicate.

Do you remember the three stories about the bear in the initial exercise? This was the basic difference. The first story uses mainly visual, the second almost exclusively auditory and the third one kinaesthetic expressions. Thus, your answer which of the three stories you liked best may offer you some essential hints about which might be your primary representational system.

Exercise: Sensory Vocabulary

Get back to the introduction and the three tales about the bear. Write down the specific sensory expressions in each. This is an excellent rehearsal to get a clear view, an open ear and a precise feeling of representational predicates.

Story 1:

Story 2:

Story 3:

There are some additional, yet not too reliable indications of the internal representational processes of a person.

Visual individuals usually turn their eyes upward when thinking about something, they are tall and slim, speak in a rapid manner, have a high voice and breathe into the chest.

Auditory people move their eyes along the middle line, are of average size and stature, talk in a normal and often melodic manner and breathe into the diaphragm.

A kinaesthetic person turns the eyes downwards (to the right) while contemplating, has either a corpulent or an athletic body, speaks slowly with a low voice and breathes deep into the belly.

Taking these characteristics into account may be very helpful to complete the verbal signals or to validate them if they are not sufficiently clear in their evidence.

What is the gain that these considerations have to offer for Energetic-Hypnosis? At first, they are important in obtaining rapport with the client. The more it is possible to meet him in his world, especially meeting his way of thinking, the more intense and complete is the feeling of trust and understanding. This is essential for successful cooperation and interaction. When knowing the primary representational system of a person, it is highly recommended to use mainly its predicates. The effect is extremely subtle and very fundamental.

But there is another fascinating feature. The subconscious mind usually runs on another modality than the primary one. Thus, it turned out to be very useful to switch the communication to the least used representational system as soon as the client enters a trance state. This supports the avoidance of the critical factors of the conscious mind because now you do no longer speak its language. Instead it has become much easier to influence the subconscious.

If there is uncertainty or no information about the primary representational system of a person, the best strategy should be to address all three modalities VAK in equal proportions. In this way one at least circumvents the danger of permanently mismatching and, thus, threat the rapport. The same is of course true if an individual uses two or three of the modalities in more or less equal shares.

5. Time Distortion

Not only Albert Einstein knew that time is relative. Also the subconscious mind is quite familiar with this dimension. It is a very common effect of hypnosis that the experience of time differs in a sometimes very dramatic way from that in normal waking state. This is quite useful to ratify the trance and, in addition, it offers a number of fascinating opportunities to create therapeutic results.

Time distortion shows up in two distinct ramifications. On the one hand, it describes the leaving of the current time frame, the 'here and now'. On the other, the experience of the length of time spans is changed in a state of trance. While the first is a standard tool of hypnotic interventions, e.g. for age regressions, the second feature is a speciality of Energetic-Hypnosis and is rarely applied otherwise.

Explicitly not in the realm of usage are trance states that aim at reaching past lives. Though it is possible, in principle, to guide a person in trance backwards through time towards ages long before the current life span. How reliable the 'memories' are that can be activated by such a procedure, is not the prime question. The opinions on that matter differ substantially. Empirical investigations that checked the details about past lives which emerged in trance, sometimes resulted in impressive accuracy and displayed knowledge that should have been impossible for the test person to posses it.

Vital is the fact that one enters a very speculative field. This is not in accordance with the scientific requirements of Energetic-Hypnosis and does not offer any apparent therapeutic value.[8]

Everybody knows that the experience of durations may differ massively even in normal waking states. Occasionally time flies while under different conditions minutes seem to last for hours.[9] The main reason is that humans do

---

8 It is not easy to comprehend in which way the knowledge about supposed events of past lives should be helpful in dealing with current problems. For example, somebody discovers that he was burned alive at a stake. The reliving of horrors like that might bear the risk of a substantial trauma that could be intense enough to devastate even the next three lives. Alternatively, imagine the opposite scenario: somebody 'remembers' a former live full of happiness and wealth while his present-day situation offers none of that. This can hardly be anything else but depressing. By the way, much more thrilling than exploring past lives seems to me the hypnotic investigation of things to come.

9 Very common is the effect that in a state of shock, e.g. during an accident, people get the impression of slow motion. Similar reports are given by individuals with near-death experiences, where the whole live seems to pass by within less than a second.

not have any sensor that is able to measure time directly. Hence, the brain is permanently forced to construct time relations. One interesting property is the spatial representation of time by the mind. This can even be recognized by common phrases: something is 'far' in the 'distant' future or lasted for a 'long' while. Yet, distance and length are of course primarily spatial attributes.

These effects permeate many areas of live. For example, when reading a book, some chapters seem much longer than others, even if they comprise the same number of pages.

The phenomenon of leaving the current time frame in hypnosis splits into two opposite directions, depending whether one heads towards future or past.

When reaching for the past, this is called age regression because of experiencing oneself taken back to earlier phases of one's individual lifetime. This is most successfully achieved by telling the hypnotic subject to move or slide backwards through time, step by step, day by day, year by year, until either it reaches the age or the year that was aimed at, or till the moment that a certain event occurred, if the exact date was not remembered any more. Instead, it is also possible to give the person the command to move straight to a certain point in the past, yet, the gradual and slow shifting of the time frame has evidenced to be preferable.

The purpose of age regression is either to add new resources to a traumatic event in the past. Resources and abilities that the person did not have at this earlier stage. This shall provoke a new and updated evaluation of that event. Of course, all the procedures that are available to deal with unpleasant experiences in the past can also be incorporated, like cognitive methods, EMDR[10] or the NLP-techniques Re-Imprint and Change-History.

Or the contrary intention is pursued, i.e. the activation of resources and skills that were once available but got lost afterwards. This is often very helpful to deal with current issues.

The intention of shifting a person towards a point of time in the future is not to be clairvoyant but to associate him or her with a future state, for example, a personal goal that is desired. On the one hand, to judge if this is actually consistent with the person's own wishes and needs and, on the other hand, to trigger off subconscious processes to reach for that goal with verve. Finally, it is possible to check from that future perspective if there might be a requirement for further resources or skills that could be helpful or necessary. In most cases, these can be found in the past of the person and, thus, be obtained from there.

---

10 Eye Movement Desensitisation and Reprocessing, developed by Francine Shapiro.

The substantially different and extremely fascinating phenomenon of altered experience of duration in hypnosis was explored intensively by Milton Erickson in his early years of research[11] but was hardly used later on, neither by Erickson himself nor by others.

This effect comprises two opposite directions, time expansion and time compression. The second effect is a very familiar one with trance subjects because they regularly underestimate the amount of time that they spent in the state of hypnosis. Though this offers excellent evidence to the client that he actually was in an altered state, there are not much further therapeutic applications besides getting over painful or unpleasant experiences fast.

Instead, the expansion of subjective time can be of use in various ways. In the state of hypnotic trance, people often experience events that last, in their view, up to several hours while actually only a few seconds have passed. The person itself does not have any sense of time lapse. Examples reach from simple counting experiments via learning and exercising to even reliving extended memories. In some cases, the rapid execution of creative top performances is documented. A very sophisticated application is giving careful chosen suggestions to rush the hypnotised person through some sequences of a hypnotic process at a massively increased rate, using the associated improvement in mental and intellectual abilities.

Exercise: Time

1. Think of time as a solid line in space that reaches from the past on one side towards the future on the other side. Now point to the direction of the past. Afterwards to the direction of the future.[12]

2. Place a huge pot of cold water on your kitchen stove and wait until it boils. Measure the time it takes. Estimate the time span before looking at your watch. How high is the relative deviation?[13]

%
____

____

11 See Cooper & Erickson (2004)

12 In most cases, you should have placed the past to the left and the future to the right of you. The reason for that is unknown. One quite plausible idea proposes a connection to the direction of writing. Hence, individuals that were raised with the opposite direction of writing (e.g. Arab) should differ in this regard, too.

13 Remember the saying: "The watched pot never boils!"?

6. Reach Your Goals

Each vividly visualized goal possess the imminent urge to become reality. The prospect of achieving a goal becomes more probable the more it is formulated in a way that satisfies certain formal requirements. These requirements are called 'criteria of well-formedness'.

Regarding Energetic-Hypnosis it is optimal if goals are formulated positively, in first person singular and in present tense. There must not be any restrictions or weakenings of the statement and, further more, an exact time frame is indicated. Finally, it is essential that goals are realistic, achievable and ecologically as well as sensory definite. We shall work out these aspects in detail soon. Besides it's always advantageous, if a target is attractive. But the effects of the formal aspects listed above are basically independent of that feature. Even targets like cleaning up or dish-washing, which are often not particularly attractive, are more likely to be implemented if they are stated in a proper way.

Literature knows various other schemes for the designing of goals. One of the most popular is known by the acronym S.M.A.R.T. and is regularly used in the business sector and with project-management. The letters mean Specific, Measurable, Attractive, Realistic and Timed. It is obvious that the content of these requirements is basically identical with those of Energetic-Hypnosis. It is important to keep in mind that the attainment of a goal is more likely if the formal description is based on certain standards.

However, to delimit are approaches that have become very popular recently, like ordering from the universe, in a way that is propagated by Bärbel Mohr's writings, the 'Secret' by Rhonda Byrne, Esther Hicks' publications or the somewhat older recommendations made by Joseph Murphy. Usually, they suggest to place a wish and then take no further action, trusting that the universe, or whoever, will grant the fulfilment. Yet, there are indeed certain overlaps with our way as the aforementioned approaches also emphasize the importance of positive wording and always work with powerful visualisations.

The fundamental difference derives from the fact that it often lacks the property of being able to reach the target by oneself. For example, think of winning the lottery. You can, of course, formulate the request and then forward it to the universe. All you are able to contribute yourself is to buy a lottery ticket. This characteristic separates 'wishes' from 'goals'. Although there certainly may be some area in-between, Energetic-Hypnosis deals primarily with the latter ones.[14]

---

14 Besides, you are strongly encouraged to try other ideas as well. My own experiments showed some amazing and surprising results.

Of course, quite naturally the question arises, whether you pursue goals or wishes by reading this book.

Well-formedness criteria

1. Positive

The goal has to be formulated without any negation. The motivational direction has to be a clearly towards it. Thus, you have to unambiguously declare what it is that you want to achieve, and not, what you want to leave or avoid.

Hence, words like 'not', 'nobody', 'never' or alike may not be included in the formulation of the target that you are aiming at. The subconscious is only able to reach for goals that can be visualised. A 'not' requires to visualise exactly that item that you want to get rid of.[15] In the worst case, this may result in a push towards the state, which you deliberately want to avoid.

In addition, 'positive' also means that no comparatives are incorporated. That means, to avoid comparisons in the way of 'more than', 'less', 'slimmer' in the formulation of the goal. Instead, only concrete and precise statements are of use.

2 First Person Singular

There must be no doubt, whose goal it is that is talked about. Only this way one will result in the highest possible impact on the subconscious to reach for it. This is only achievable if the term 'I' is used as the subject of a sentence. Constructions like 'It should...' or 'The goal is...' have to be avoided. Also, the common phrases 'You' or 'One' when talking about oneself are not helpful. It is your goal that you are talking about. This has to be absolutely clear and unambiguous. As you might remember, the subconscious operates extremely literal.

3. Present Tense

Goals have to be stated in the present and not, like most of the times, in future tense. The exact neurological or psychological mechanisms are not really known but, regarding this point, so-called positive thinking and the above-mentioned approaches actually had lots of fruitful influence. They all suggest that the target is to be expressed in a way as if it is already reality.

---

15 To get the point, it is often recommended not to think of a blue elephant. Inevitably, you first have to imagine exactly this blue elephant in order to subsequently 'not' think of it.

It is suggested that so-called cognitive dissonance might play a part. This describes the situation that experienced reality and believe do not fit. The brain dislikes such a state and aims at changing it by bringing both into accordance. Thus the effect of goal orientation is only pronounced when the brain is signalled that the aim is already reached. Often, however, the use of 'will be' has the consequence that the target is seen as something in the future for all times. It lurks the well-known 'cows-come-home-day-effect'.

4. No Weakening

The goal has to be absolutely straight. Use of the subjunctive like 'should' 'could', 'would', or the incorporation of verbs like 'want', 'desire', 'intend', 'try' are as counterproductive as the phrases 'perhaps', 'approximately', 'possibly'. All this weakens the importance of the objective for you. Your subconscious is sensitive to the highest degree to such plasticisers and accordingly reduces the priority of the accompanied target.

If you are not sure whether you actually should aim at your target, there might be perfectly good reasons for doubting. It is highly recommended to deal with possible (subconscious) impediments. There is no use in trying to avoid this confrontation because, in this case, you will have very little chances to actually reach your goals.

5. Exact Time-Frame

There has to be a precise date for the implementation of the goal. Of course, one that is realistic and achievable. Even if the target is not completely reached by that day, it shall be quite easy then to set a new date because of the experiences gained meanwhile. Anyway, this risk is small and negligible compared to the disadvantages of completely skipping it. Also, the use of vague expressions like 'in the near future', 'soon', 'within the next weeks' or 'someday' is risky, because the already mentioned 'cows-come-home-day-effect' is almost guaranteed.

Should the definition of a specific target date prove exceptionally difficult, one can instead resort to the formulation 'not later then date xy'. With very complex challenges, there exists the option to split them into smaller sub-goals, for which the time horizon can be estimated more easily.

6. Realistic

In addition to the already mentioned distinction between 'wishes', which are mainly dependent on fate, chance or other persons, and 'goals', it is also important to note whether something, that is quite feasible in principle, might be outside the realm of capabilities or skills of a certain person. Successful participation at next year's triathlon at Hawaii can be quite realistic for a thirty year old person. Whether this is also true for someone in his early eighties, suffering from substantial overweight and serious heart problems, might be rather questionable. Therefore, it varies individually what is realistic and what isn't. But ultimately, it always has to be left to each person what he or she believes possible.

7. Sensory Definiteness[16]

This describes the property of a goal to be in some way identifiable and verifiable with the help of one's own five senses.

This can be achieved by direct experience (one 'sees' the desired car in the garage, 'feels' the holiday sun on the skin, 'hears' the wedding bells) or indirectly on the basis of the usually visually registered indicators or measuring devices (e.g. scales, bank statements, reports).

8. Ecology

One of the most important criteria for objectives is their 'ecology'. This implies that the achievement must actually be useful for the person or at least not in contrary to the individual character, the well-being, the personal values or other important goals. In addition, the implementation must also fit the social environment.

These two aspects are not only a requirement of psycho hygiene but also have the quite simple reasoning. A goal that does not meet these requirements, will have little prospect of being achievable. At least, not for a very long time. Because there will be very massive internal and external resistances that are likely to sabotage the outcome in many ways.

In order to check the ecology, it is necessary to envision oneself vividly in the desired state. All senses should be incorporated to make the experience of that goal as complete as possible. Associated in this way, it is important to elicit carefully whether everything is perfect or if reservations or a feeling of unease do appear. Furthermore, any important private or business relation has to be taken into account. Examine, what consequences are to be expected.

Once again, it is recommended that this step has to be performed with as much care as possible, neither hasty nor superficial. If it happens that ecology

---

16 The somewhat odd but common notion of definiteness derives from linguistics and does mean that the relationship between a word and the object in the real world, which it describes, has to be identifiable and/or unique. In our context it is hence required that the realization of a target has to be identifiable and/or unique (for the sensory perception).

problems or obstacles arise, they are absolutely legitimate and serve to avoid future serious setbacks. In general, the consequence is not to discard the goal completely. Usually, it only requires some minor adjustments or some additional consideration in order to reach an absolutely fine situation.

An interesting side effect of this intense sensory perception of the achieved goal is the emotional power that goes along with it. This charges the subconscious with high energy towards reaching the goal. Much more pronounced than the mere visualisation of a target in the way that is recommended by many alternative techniques.

Exercise: Goals

1. Choose a personal goal that is not too ambitious, in order to be able to check the success after one week. Design the goal step by step, according to the eight well-formedness criteria.

2. At the end of the week check whether you were able to realize the goal, and to what extent. If you haven't reached it, think about the possible reasons for that failure.

3. Now choose a more important objective and formulate it according to these eight well-formedness criteria. Regularly check your progress regarding implementation and achievement.

Goals and Resources in the context of Energetic-Hypnosis

The correct formulation of objectives has to be discussed with the client before the beginning of the hypnosis. This ensures that appropriate suggestions are used during the trance.

However, the review of the ecology is carried out best during the trance and forms a vital part of any hypnotic work. The intense mental association with the future state allows the subject to fully assess whether the implementation will truly be beneficial for the whole personality and for the relevant social environment. As a consequence, this allows to perform a much more rigorous eco-check than could be achieved in the waking state.

Furthermore, the opportunity is given to examine whether the activation of additional resources is helpful or even necessary. The common approach used by Energetic-Hypnosis is to ask the client to dissociate from the target image. This is best done by imagining to be looking at oneself from above. From that perspective it is quite easy to judge which abilities or characteristics are still missing in order to grant an even more perfect or more simple path towards reaching the goal. As soon as these are identified, the client is requested to slide back through time mentally in the way that was described as age regression in the chapter about time distortion.

The clear call to trace the individual history to find an experience or a memory, in which the requested resource already has been available, should regularly result in a success. From there it will be taken back to the future and integrated into the target. This should produce an alteration and an enrichment of the desired situation. The client is asked to enjoy this progress as intense as possible and with all senses before the procedure is repeated. This goes on as long and as often as is necessary to reach ultimate satisfaction.

7. Six-Step-Reframing

Six-Step Reframing was developed in its basic form in the early days of NLP by Richard Bandler and John Grinder. Meanwhile, various subtypes and variants have been created, with a broad range of proposed sequential parts and sometimes quite strange modifications of the individual steps. Some might have primarily served the purpose of increasing the author's prestige and the sales of his publications, but did not add anything important or new.

Anyway, this methodology is indicated whenever a client suffers from an unwanted behaviour or a recurrent pattern that operates against his expressed wishes. The aim is in any case to separate this troublesome behaviour, step by step, from the underlying positive intention. Subsequently an improved new and better way to meet this intention shall be implemented.

The six steps (which are all essential for a lasting success):

1. Contact with the problematic part

2. Separation of behaviour and intention

3. Detecting the highest positive intention

4. Creating alternatives

5. Eco-Check

6. Future Pace

The concept of reframing stems originally from Virginia Satir's family therapy but was also used by Milton Erickson in many cases. Essentially, its purpose is to take a negative behaviour or experience and offer a different meaning or a new context in which it exhibits positive aspects.

The notion that the personality of a client consists of several parts which produce one or more of the unwanted behaviours, may seem somewhat hideous at first glance. But this is merely a conceptual model. It is not important whether it is true or realistic, but whether it is helpful and effective.

Since Energetic-Hypnosis is interested in the usefulness of an approach in the course of personal development, questions like that are not really interesting anyway. By the way, the idea of human personality consisting of various parts is not really new because even in Freud's model of the human psyche you find the different and partially contradictory structures 'Superego', 'I' and 'It'.

The six steps in detail

<u>1. Contact with the problem part</u>

Once the undesired behaviour is defined, that part of the clients personality, which produces this behaviour, is addressed. This is done in a light trance. Already the contact with an internal part of personality should by itself lead into an altered state of consciousness anyway.

Whether communication from now on is carried out verbally or via so-called ideomotoric signalling (e.g. head nod or finger signals), is of lesser importance. The former displays the disadvantage that talking might disturb the hypnotic state and is, thus, not favoured by many clients.

Sometimes it is recommended to give the part a name or to visualise it (with shape, colour, etc.) or to imagine to take it out of the body. Such subtleties are by no means necessary as elements of the Energetic-Hypnosis and might seem rather grotesque to some people. All in all, it is up to the therapist and the client and their preferences regarding special-fx.

It is crucial to communicate with the part in a respectful way. It has to be thanked not only for the willingness to cooperate but it also should be indicated that it is known that it pursues an absolutely positive and important task. In addition, it is to be insured that everything that might be altered, will happen only with its explicit consent. It is exclusively up to the parts final decision whether any change may occur. This is the only way to prevent that the problem part (which you should of course never address this way) terminates at some point the interaction and cooperation.

<u>2. Separation of intention from behaviour</u>

Once communication has been established, the part will be asked to share its positive intention.

Again, this can even be done verbally but it seems to be favourable to leave this to the client and simply let him indicate that the part gave him the information. This has the tremendous advantage that the client does not have to report any intimate, maybe surprising or even embarrassing personal details to another person. And for the process itself it is completely irrelevant whether the therapist gets any information about the content.

<u>3. Detecting the highest positive intention</u>

Very often, there are even deeper intentions hidden behind the first communicated one. It is therefore merely a (first) intermediate goal which still serves important purposes. Therefore, the aim of the next question to be asked is to elicit whether the intention revealed covers another purpose behind it. In this case, the part is asked to disclose this one as well and indicate that.

This procedure is reiterated until the declared highest positive intention is discovered. How many iterations are necessary varies from person to person dramatically. But even with the same person, this my differ depending on the topic in question. In rare cases the highest positive intention is already found after the first round. On the other hand, sometimes the cycle is repeated dozens of times without any prospect to terminate. In such cases, it is advisable to give the part the direct order to get to the absolute highest intention immediately. Even then, it usually takes a few further passes. The instance that an end is never reached and, instead, no other choice is left except cancelling the procedure altogether fortunately appears almost never.

Once the highest positive intention is eventually revealed, the part is questioned whether it actually achieves this with the previous behaviour. In most cases the answer will be, "No!". But even if the question should be answered with a "Yes!", which happens from time to time, the part is usually happy to accept the prospect to receive some additional alternatives to realize its aim. Because it is always preferable to have a choice than to have none. Finally, the part is given thanks once again for its support.

4. Creating alternatives

The 4th step affords to turn to a creative part of the personality of the client and ask this one to generate five new behavioural alternatives that meet the highest positive intention at least as good (or even much better than) as the previous unwanted activity. Even at this point, it is not necessary that the coach is informed, what these alternatives comprise in detail. It is sufficient that the client shows that the search for these five alternatives is completed.

Next, the original part is contacted again and instructed to display sequentially for each of the five new alternatives whether this was in its interest and should be applied henceforth. Regularly, there will be at least one of them that is to be discarded. It is excellent if that happens at this stage as it will prevent the otherwise inevitably occurrence of intrapersonal conflicts that might threaten the overall success. And it ensures that the behavioural changes are really supported. Explicitly affirmed variants cause also a very intense commitment.

If there are at least three of the new options accepted, this step is completed. Otherwise, we turn again to the creative part with the invitation to produce more ideas in order to reach the minimum number of three.[17] Thought in principle this procedure could be repeated, if the new alternatives are rejected once more, this usually does not make much since. For in general this indicates that there are deeper objections that should be addressed first. Fortunately, it happens almost never that after two iterations the minimum number is not reached.

5. Eco-Check

Now it is important to clarify whether the changes are really ecological, i.e. useful for the whole client. This is ensured by checking whether there are other parts within his personality that have reservations against the new way.

It is perfectly legitimate and appropriate if such objections are raised at this point because it has to be assumed that these critical parts are pursuing good and noble intentions as well. To not appreciate them adequately, might have the consequence that they would show up later in one way or another and probably cause complete failure of the desired changes.

If there are concerns, one approach is to ask whether additional resources are required and then to insert them. Often, it is sufficient to arrange a trial period of several weeks, during which the new behaviour might be applied without being disturbed. If, however, nothing is successful, it is wise to return to step 4 and repeat from there on.

6. Future Pace

The final step is to transfer the success into the future and to create a conditioned response. If this is neglected, there is the risk that the progress achieved may remain stuck in the present instead of transforming the ongoing life.

In order to achieve this, the client is asked to put himself into the future mentally to a point in time, at which the new behaviour has already been realized since quite a while. Next, it is required to imagine as vividly and intensively as possible, how it will be to have achieved this goal. Each of the representational systems should be addressed at length in order to make the experience really effective.

This completes the process and the client is reoriented to the 'Here and Now'.

---

17 The idea behind this number is the opinion of Richard Bandler that in the case of only a single choice one has to operate like a robot. With two alternatives to choose from, you are in a dilemma. At least three options are required to get some freedom of choice.

Exercise: Six-Step-Reframing

1. Take one of your behaviours that bothers you. Relax a bit and apply the six steps.

2. Ask a friend to operate as a client with his own issue and apply this technique.

8. Metaphors

The basic concept of a metaphor[18] is to translate an event from one context into another and, thus, to address multiple levels of meaning and communication. This offers a very sophisticated way to deal with possible resistance and allows to communicate with the subconscious mind in a disguised manner. This approach has proven to be very successful especially for highly rational and extremely critical individuals.

The idea of using metaphors to convey information isn't really new. For example, the parables in the New Testament, which Jesus used frequently, are very similar. Also the fables of Aesop are quite alike. Moreover, everyone knows this form of communication from the everyday life in the form of puns and analogies.

The creation and the purpose of a metaphor is somewhat like taking an offshoot of a stunted garden plant to the balcony in order to try and see if it needs more resources, such as more fertilizer or other light conditions. Of course, with the actual aim of using the lessons learned this way in order to bring the original flower in the garden to thrive and prosper.

In a similar way, the therapeutic use of metaphors allows to distract the consciousness of the listener in order to bypass the so-called critical factor. Thus, the subconscious potentials can be addressed directly. This enables one to activate resources or to find solutions, which were not accessible on the conscious level so far.

What is to be taken into account with regard to constructing a metaphor? What is important in order to reach the therapeutic goals as completely as possible?[19]

The main principle in the designing of metaphors is called 'isomorphism'.[20] That is, the real events are transferred to a completely different setting, which is of similar structure. This may be a fairy tale, a fable, or an invented or real event with existing human beings. The table illustrates the similarities between the metaphor and the real events in a therapeutic setting.

---

18 Greek 'metà: somewhere else, phérein': carry

19 One of the best presentations regarding metaphors is Gordon (2005).

20 Greek 'isomorph': of equal shape

Real Event	Metaphor
Client	Protagonist
Person 1	Character 1
⋮	⋮
Event 1	Incident 1
⋮	⋮
Problem	Solution

Table: Isomorphism

It is important to avoid a reference too obvious to the life of the target person. In that case, the intention to start subconscious processes within the listener, that will often take days or even weeks, is thwarted. Because the conscious mind notices what is going on and might object the proposed ideas.

There exist especially two devices to increase the impact that a metaphor will have on the audience, yet, remain subliminal enough to avoid conscious perception with certainty: the Satir categories and the representational systems. Both are used to design the main characters of the story.

Satir Categories

The trained observer will notice very quickly, which of the four modes of reaction described by Virginia Satir is the typical one the a specific client exhibits. Even what is the preferred sensory channel.

More challenging is the classification of other persons involved in the events. In most cases, these are not personally known to the coach, so only the client's statements can serve as a source of information. Yet, this is often a minor problem in practice as, actually, it does not really matter whether the persons are described adequately and in fact behave in that way in real life. Crucial is the idea that resides in the mind of the client.

This information can be very useful to vest the characters in the story with the appropriate qualities and behaviours of their real counterparts.

The following table shows an overview of the verbal and nonverbal behaviours that are typical for the respective Satir category.

	Blamer	**Placater**	**Computer**	**Distractor**
Attitude	threatening	excusing	rational	confused
Voice	loud	silent	monotone	unsteady
Verbal Patterns	- Universals: everybody, all, always, never, nobody - Imperative: have to, must not, ought to	- Limitations: if, merely, only, rather - Subjunctive: would, could, should	- 'Ego'-Deletion: it is, one, somebody - Nominalisations	- sudden changes of the topic discussed - evading answers

Table: Satir Categories

Representational Systems

The second notable aspect is the preferred sensory channel, especially one of the three main variants VAK.

In the chapter on the representational systems has been mentioned that the associated properties go far beyond the mere use of the respective terminology. These are indeed only audible expression of the kind of thinking that is typical for an individual. And in a remarkable way, this often affects even the physique. One can speculate about the kind of interactions or the direction of causality that generated these results, but more relevant is the use in the designing process of the protagonists of the metaphor. The following table provides an overview.

	Visual	**Auditory**	**Kinaesthetic**
Predicates	see	hear	feel
Physiognomy	tall, slim	average	Stocky or athletic
Voice	high, talking fast	average, rhythmic	low, slow
Breathing	chest	diaphragm	belly

Table: Representational Systems

These two schemes are not independent, for e.g. blamers often tend to be primarily visual. Computers are usually auditory and placaters kinaesthetic. However, the correlation is not very strict, therefore, it is a good advise to pay attention to both.

These consideration are extremely valuable with respect to creating solutions. Skilfully transferring the sensory-specific predicates of the characters to a common modality can contribute substantially to the resolution of a conflict. Especially, regarding problems that stem from communication discrepancies. In many instances, misunderstandings arise because the persons involved have different primary representational systems. Hence, they literally live in different worlds and constantly miss each other in conversations even if they actually talk about the same topic or share the identical opinion.

The most elaborated way to switch from one sensory channel to another is the utilization of a particular phenomenon of the human brain, the so-called Synaesthesia.

Exercise: Synaesthesia 1

1. Below are two drawn figures. One is called 'Kiki', the other 'Buba'. Attach the names.

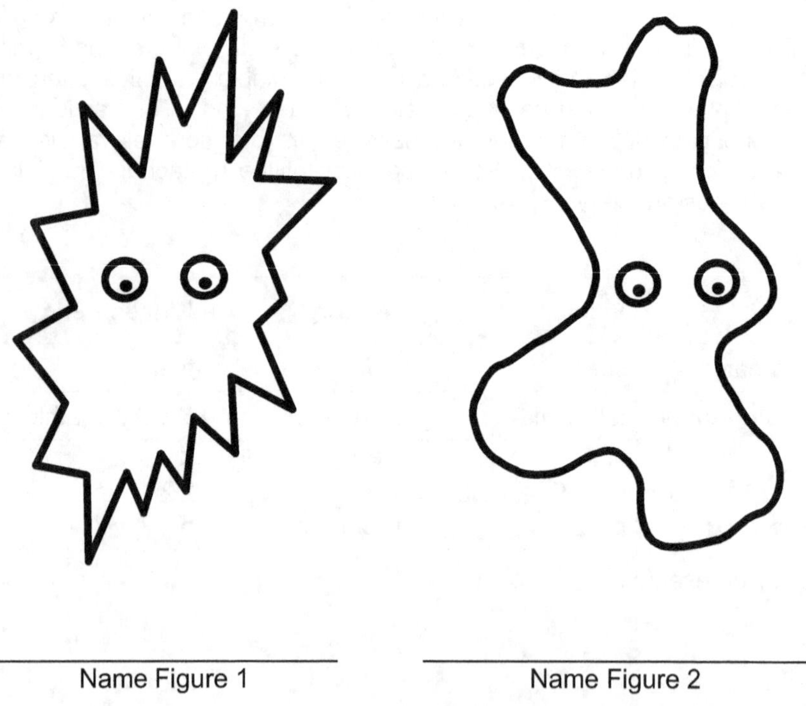

| Name Figure 1 | Name Figure 2 |

2. What are the reasons for your decision? Why didn't you do it the other way round?

____

____

____

____

____

In fact, almost all people choose the names in such a way that the sharp figure 1 receives the name Kiki while the plump figure 2 is called Buba. Needless to say that sounds have no geometric properties and, hence, there really should be no a priori reason, why the assignment differs significantly from an even partition. But the human brain obviously makes that kind of connections across different representational systems.

Studies have shown that such links exist between particular colours, pitches and temperatures. This is also reflected in everyday language. For example, the colour red is attributed as warm. Low tones are also generally associated with warmth and dark colours. Similar synesthetic connections exist between shape, texture and sound patterns. As in the exercise, round forms are associated with soft(!) sounds.

To illustrate the use of this property, let us take two opponents of a conflict, like a marriage dispute. The husband is a typical visual person, the wife of pronounced kinaesthetic orientation. It is therefore recommended that both eventually meet on neutral ground, in this case the auditory system.

In a simple example, the metaphorical representative of the husband initially uses many visual predicates and at some point shifts to auditory words. This is done most gently by using a synaesthetical transition. First, he talks about his red car and then of the low hum of its engine. The representative of the women in the metaphor, however, steps on a sharp stone and then initiates a shrill scream. From there on, they both interact by means of auditory expressions and find a good solution for their dispute.

Another important area of application with Energetic-Hypnosis is to use nested loops of metaphorical stories as a means of trance induction and installation of subconscious suggestions.

Exercise: Synaesthesia 2

1. Think of at least three more synaesthetic groups:

____

____

____

____

2. Create more short synaesthetic transitions:

a.   Visual → Kinaesthetic

____

____

____

b.   Auditory → Kinaesthetic

____

____

____

c.	Auditory → Visual

____

____

____

____

d.	Kinaesthetic → Visual

____

____

____

____

9. The Hypnotic Process

If it is not possible to get a client into a trance, that's a pity.
If it is not possible to get a client out of a trance, that's a disaster.

A typical Energetic-Hypnosis session consists of preliminary briefing, intro, suggestive part and extro. The intro marks the transition into the trance. The suggestive part is the section, in which the actual work takes place in a state of trance.

The trance itself my reaches different depths, depending on the client and the phase of the hypnotic process. Usually, a three-stage model is used that distinguishes between light, moderate and somnambulistic[21] trance:

Trance-Depth	Phenomenon
light	- relaxation - feeling of heaviness - catalepsy - reduced awareness of the environment
moderate	- reduced pain - number block - further reduced awareness of the environment - focus on internal processes
somnambulistic	- no awareness of the environment - post-hypnotic suggestions - hallucinations - amnesia

Table: Trance-Stages

---

21 Though this literally means 'sleepwalking' (Latin 'somnus': sleep, and 'ambulare': wander), the expression is now commonly used in this context.

The light form describes a condition characterised by relaxation, a heavy feeling in the eyelids and the catalepsy[22] of individual muscles. The environment is still perceived, even though the focus of attention is not on it.

In moderate trance, the surrounding recedes much further but can still be experienced. Instead, internal processes, images, sounds and memories are at the centre of attention. The perception of pain is reduced markedly and the memory of numbers is blocked.

In the state of somnambulism, finally, the outside world is no longer consciously experienced. Complex post-hypnotic suggestions are possible, including hallucinations and amnesia.
The final of the hypnotic process is the return to the normal waking state, the so-called extro. While the intro represents the greatest challenge to the skills and the flexibility of the hypnotist, the extro is the most important part.

Preliminary Briefing

Prior to the hypnotic endeavour, the hypnotist and the client should engage in some interaction to establish rapport, which is a harmonious connection between individuals that creates a strong sense of confidence. It typically exists between persons who are alike in appearance, behaviour, gestures, facial expressions and also on a verbal level.[23] The hypnotist achieves this by mirroring and pacing the client in the above aspects discreetly and quietly.

The second task of this conversation is to explicitly agree upon the goal of the meeting and to formulate the aim according to the well-formedness criteria. Additionally, the approval of the client for the following hypnosis is to be obtained, especially the allowance for possible physical contact. This of course affords detailed explanations of the Energetic-Hypnosis process.

At the same time, this offers an excellent opportunity to convey various expectations regarding the hypnotic process and to eliminate several deceptive notions about hypnosis itself. For example, it is recommended to explain that trance is something familiar and very much alike the state right before falling asleep or immediately after awakening. It should also be pointed out that the client will be aware of everything around him during hypnosis, at least initially.

----

22 Greek 'katálēpsis': immobility

23 Modern neurophysiology assigns this effect to the so-called mirror-neurons that where discovered in 1995 by Giacomo Rizzolatti. These special neurons permanently observe if and to what extent our own behaviour matches that of our fellow human beings.

It is also quite important at that stage to explain that the hypnotist will give instructions that will lead the client into a trance and enable him to make the agreed changes, but the decision about compliance is still and always in the realm of the responsibility of the client.

The arrangement of ideomotoric finger signals for communication during the trance state is optional. Also not mandatory, but very effective, are so-called 'convincers', i.e. techniques that are intended to persuade the subject of his suggestibility and subconscious responsiveness.[24]

Immediately after this briefing that must not last more than 15 minutes,[25] follows the initiation of the trance state.

Intro

Since hypnosis inherently is a transition into an altered state, it is necessary to use routines that accompany this. The methods used for the intro a known as induction techniques.

Basic approach of Energetic-Hypnosis is to use things that work and have proven to be the most successful applications in practice. Therefore, it is not surprising to find inspiration in an eclectic fashion within different approaches, especially, as the induction techniques require the highest level of flexibility on the part of the hypnotist. Human beings differ in many regards and, thus, sometimes methods remain completely without effect that usually lead to outstanding results in other instances.

The two basic methodological roots used in Energetic-Hypnosis are the permissive style in the tradition of Milton H. Erickson and the procedures of Dave Elman with its directive instruments. Although these two techniques appear incompatible at first glance, a flexible combination of the two approaches leads to above-average success in practice. The respective weights depends partly on the phase of the induction process and, of course, substantially on the personality of the client (and the hypnotist!).

---

24 An effective example of a convincer will be presented in the transcript.

25 A prolonged preliminary discussion is entirely a consequence of various strategies on the clients side in order to mask, with often highly creative means, their fear of hypnosis. If you recognize that mechanism, this should be addressed directly and/or it may be stated that the time for the client obviously is not yet ripe to engage in a trance. Everything else is a waste of time, with no prospect of a meaningful result.

In addition, there exist various other techniques of induction. For example, the famous pendulum, the various pattern interrupts, shock inductions of stage hypnosis, Estabrook's test induction or the historical strokes of Mesmer. Some of these are merely variations of the former two concepts. Anyway, it is useful and recommend to know a wide range of different styles.

Erickson

Milton Hyland Erickson (1901-1981) developed and used a tremendous and rich variety of sometimes extremely subtle techniques that are beyond the scope of this book. The many ramifications are also not necessary in the practical application and, thus, are reserved to specialists. Since Energetic-Hypnosis is a fundamentally open and expandable system, all these extensions can be incorporated. Beginners should concentrate on the basics and practice them properly. Otherwise, the result is mainly confusion instead of benefit.

The basis of each successful induction is the voice of the hypnotist. First, make sure to speak only when the client breathes out. This can be accomplished very easily if the hypnotist synchronizes his breath with the rhythm of the client's. The great additional benefit of matching the client's breathing is a tremendously positive impact on the rapport between the two individuals. Especially, the breathing frequency in this context possesses a prominent role and is also one of the most subtle ones at hand.

The second important aspect is to speak with command mode, i.e. to lower the voice towards the end of a sentence. The content of the sentence does not necessarily have to be a command in the strict sense. Rather, this type of talking (sometimes called 'downwards inflection') exhibits a tiring effect anyway, almost regardless of what is said.

Since the goal of induction is to shift the focus of attention of the client more and more from the outside world toward internal processes, one often uses the so-called 3-2-1 method. Initially, three external perceptions are linked to an internal one. Then, two external stimuli are combined with two inner perceptions and ultimately only one stimulus from the outside is referred to. Further on only internal experiences are addressed. External stimuli comprise sounds (e.g., the ticking of a clock), feelings (such as the temperature in the room), visual stimuli (such as a painting on the wall), in short, anything that the client can detect in the environment currently with one of his five senses.

Internal perceptions are, on the one hand, processes like breathing or heartbeat or feelings inside the body, on the other hand, internal pictures and images. The attention should be directed towards them as soon as a client closes the eyes.

Of course, the hypnotist can never know exactly, what the other person actually perceives. Thus, all statements are to be made in combination with vague terms such as 'possibly', 'perhaps', 'maybe', 'could', etc. Moreover, the sentences should be connected using conjunctions like 'and', 'while', 'when', 'after' and 'because'. The latter already displays a mild suggestive effect.

Exercise: Perception

1. Think of three external stimuli from your current environment (one visual, one auditory and one kinaesthetic).

____

____

____

2. Think of three current internal stimuli.

____

____

____

3. Take the three external stimuli and add one of the internal perceptions by a causal conjunction. Next, do the same thing with two outside and two internal stimuli. Finally, one external stimulus with three internal stimuli. Do it in the artfully vague manner described above.

____

____

____

____

Elman

Dave Elman (1900 - 1967) was born as the son of a stage hypnotist. Thus, already as a child he had contact with the subject of hypnosis and soon developed a very effective and rapid induction which occurs in the basic structure as described in the following.

First, the client is asked to inhale deeply, to stop the air for a short period and, eventually, to close his eyes while exhaling. This will cause a feeling of relaxation in the eyelids which is expanded to the entire body by means of appropriate suggestions.

Next, the subject is prepared to open his eyes briefly as soon as he receives the command 'now'. He opens his eyes and is immediately prompted to close them again. This eye closure is supported and accompanied by the hand of the hypnotist moving downwards along the body with two outstretched fingers at a distance of about 8 inches in front of the client. This sequence is repeated two or three times until the client is obviously no longer able to open his eyes when given the command.

Now it is announced that one arm of the client will be raised about 12 inches by the wrist. The client should let the arm absolutely loose. Thus, it will fall down again limp after letting go. This is accompanied by appropriate suggestions that the dropping of the arm shall deepen the relaxation further.

Finally, the relaxation of the mind is added to the physical relaxation. Elman used to instruct the client to slowly count out loud from '100' backwards. And even before the number '98' will be reached, all the numbers will have disappeared completely from the mind and it will become totally empty.

Exercise: Elman

1. Apply the Elman induction as self-hypnosis. Tell yourself in advance to wake up after 10 minutes.

Synthesis

Energetic-Hypnosis combines these two variants in the way that, at first, it establishes an intense rapport via the 3-2-1 method and uses it to deepen the trance until a pleasant and relaxed state is achieved. Once the eye closure is done, the Elman procedures are implemented.

The repeated opening and closing of the eyes causes a fractioning of the trance state because each time the client is brought out of it to some degree. But this results in a significant deepening of the hypnosis subsequently. The use of exactly this effect is the main basis for the efficiency of Energetic-Hypnosis. Not all aspects of Elman's basic scheme are always used, however. Both, the lifting of the arm and the loud counting is suitable only in exceptional cases and is usually not necessary at all. In contrast, the means of an explicit relaxation of the mind should always be incorporated in one way or another, with the help of appropriate suggestions.

So-called experts have been debating dogmatically for several decades whether the permissive or the authoritarian style is the right one. Apart from the fact that one often gets the impression that theoretical discussions were conducted primarily by persons with little or no practical experience, the best recommendation is to try yourself what works best for you. As mentioned earlier, not only the character of the client is crucial also the personality and current mood of the hypnotist are important determinants. Some are just more comfortable with one method instead of another. There is nothing wrong with that. Both approaches have their merits and their justification. And both work equally well in principle, depending on the context. Far more crucial than the procedure used is the fact that the hypnotist is authentic in his work and unambiguously takes the lead in the relationship.

Suggestive Part

Once the client is in a sufficiently deep trance state, the actual work begins. Now, the techniques described in the previous chapters are employed: the insertion of resources, the Six-Step-Reframing, time-distortion and metaphors. In addition, direct behavioural instructions are given. Both, in terms of actions within the hypnosis, for example, levitation of the arms or further trance deepening, as well as with respect to post-hypnotic responses, in particular partial amnesia.

Extro

After all hypnotic work is carried out, the time has come for the extro. As noted at the beginning, this is basically the most important section of the trance, which affords the greatest care. The failure of the induction which happens even to the most experienced hypnotists from time to time, might be regrettable, yet, no great harm is caused.

However, if the trance state is not dissolved completely, the consequences might be dramatic. The lesser problem is when someone does not respond at all. Probably the person has simply fallen asleep. Thus, it is up to the hypnotist and his schedule whether he lets the client continue to slumber or simply wakes him up gently or less gently.

If, instead, the client is in very deep trance, one should continue with the waking suggestions with some more emphasis until the appropriate responses appear. Alternatively, one can simply leave the person in hypnosis. By the time the bladder or something alike demands its right, the person will regain consciousness. The frequently expressed fear that they may never come out of trance is a myth. That simply does not happen.

The real danger is that the client is apparently completely returned to the waking state but is actually still in a dim condition and primarily captured by his internal operations and impressions. Or maybe even pulse and blood pressure are very low. This is often not easily detectable from the outside, especially for the beginner. The importance of complete removal of the trance becomes obvious in considering a client will afterwards participate in street traffic, possibly as driver of a vehicle.

Technically the extro is basically a mirroring of the intro, thus, the hypnotist speaks when the client inhales, and raises his voice towards the end of the sentences. The voice should now be noticeably louder and more determined than before.

Also, the client is reoriented to the environment, i.e his attention is guided more and more towards external stimuli. In addition, counting techniques are used, for example, in the simple manner, "I will now count from one to three. With every number you will wake up a bit more. Once I say 'Three', you shall open your eyes and return fully to the 'Here and Now'. You will feel awake and refreshed like after a long night's sleep!".

As soon as the client opens his eyes, he is asked to stretch, look around and drink a few sips of water till the reorientation in the present circumstances is completely regained. Especially for clients who have arrived by their car, it is a very good idea to recommend to take a walk around the block before they get behind the wheel. Safety first!

A special advice is to interview the clients at the end, what changes in their feelings they can comprehend now. On the one hand, it diverts the attention from dealing with the previous hypnosis, which would always be highly counterproductive. The coach should stop all the approaches that might go in that direction immediately. On the other hand, the client is granted an impression of the progress that has already been achieved by now.

10. Self-Hypnosis

In contrast to using the services of a hypnotist, self-hypnosis posses certain benefits and disadvantages. On the one hand, there are no schedule restrictions. You can apply it whenever there is sufficient time and a quiet place. But it has to be accepted that during the trance state there is no external companion to react flexible whenever current events and needs demanded for it. Also, it is hardly possible to support complex processes, such as Six-Step-Reframing or inserting resources in a similar relaxed and deep state of hypnosis. And it shall be more difficult to offer the optimal suggestions.

Less important is the difference with respect to the accessible trance-depth. For, with a little experience, one is able to reach the identical stages by oneself, even somnambulism. It should be noted that particularly in this extraordinary state of the mind the presence of a hypnotist would be particularly effective, though. Only an external person may be able to provide the perfectly adequate suggestions. This simply cannot be done by oneself in deep trance.

Also, the sequence of the hypnotic process differs in some aspects. Instead of the preliminary briefing, you apply a kind of self-analysis of the purpose that shall be achieved within the subsequent self-hypnosis. This should be accomplished preferably in written form because this affords a more intensive and verifiable way and, additionally, offers more impact on the following process. The intentions may reach from a mere relaxation without further suggestions to very complex internal processes, like the anchoring of goals,[26] or adding supportive auto-suggestions.

Following the detailed examination of the intentions of the upcoming self-hypnosis, the goals and purposes of the ensuing trance are communicated to the own subconscious in a relaxed position and in a respectful manner. If necessary, the time of the termination of the trance experience is communicated in an explicit way to the subconscious. Usually the subconscious is impressively precise in that regard. Of course one can also use an alarm clock. For it is not very helpful for relaxation, tranquillity and serenity if there are scheduling concerns.

After these preparations, the induction process may begin. In the previous chapter you have already gathered some experience by means of the Elman exercise. That was a so-called blank hypnosis because you just dipped into a trance and did not add any change work or suggestions. I recommend trying different approaches. To find out, what works best for you, and on the other hand, to acquire a high degree of flexibility and choices.

---

26 Already formulated in accordance with the well-formedness criteria.

In particular, the 3-2-1-induction is perfectly suitable for the beginner to guide oneself inwards. The perception exercise in the previous chapter provides the basis.

Now, you will devote yourself more and more to the subconscious processes as conscious control fades. Depending on the depth of trance one reaches, it might still be possible to be aware of what is going on and, thus, be able to consciously control what is happening. The subconscious is now prepared to implement the previously requested steps autonomously.

Eventually, the extro is accomplished without necessarily influence and guidance from an outside person. Therefore, the warnings from the previous section are warranted once more. Make sure that you really have left the trance state completely. Please support this with explicitly worded prompts that you sent to yourself, even if you are apparently awake. Stretch, breathe deeply, drink a few sips of water and move in fresh air. Especially, if you are going to drive a car or operate machinery. This cannot be overstressed.

In a chapter about self-hypnosis there should also be some notes about hypnosis CDs and audio files. Such products are offered on almost every imaginable issue. And they enjoy increasing popularity. In many cases, they may actually be quite helpful and they are very easy to use. However, the quality of the sold goods varies considerably. The main disadvantage is the complete lack of flexibility with respect to the individual listener's needs, both, in terms of the induction process and, even more, with regard to the given suggestions. Therefore, they rarely attain the results that the suppliers promise. Disappointments are almost certain and, all too often, this unpleasant experience will not be blamed on the specific product but on the method of hypnosis in general.

More suitable seem self-produced recordings. Because the individual knows better of the own needs and preferences and is able to account for them. However, due to lack of experience and knowledge, especially the beginner in this area often fails to provide the necessary professionalism to achieve really effective results. At worst, it can even unintentionally cause counterproductive or harmful effects.

A particular problem with self-hypnosis exhibit the so-called 'blind spots'. It is the key to successful self development that precisely the often painful aspects that you want to hide from yourself and avoid to deal with, are addressed. This can only be achieved by empathetic and competent intervention from outside. This ensures that an eye is on the very aspects that promise to show the most lasting effect.

The best and most reliable recommendation is, therefore, to turn to an experienced and qualified hypnotist. This guarantees to be introduced into the possibilities of hypnosis in a controlled and safe environment. Hence, you will receive training under professional guidance in order to obtain optimal results and learn all the complex specifics of self-hypnosis.

11. Questionnaire

One secret of the effectiveness and efficiency of a typical Energetic-Hypnosis session is the fact that the intervention has already started way before the client enters the office.

How is this possible? Because the client receives and returns a carefully designed questionnaire a few days earlier.

This serves the purpose of intense engagement with the upcoming issue in advance. The questions are chosen in a way to activate new perspectives and so far unconsidered aspects. Beyond that, it even offers valuable insights into the special structure of the problem and the personality of the client to the coach. For example, it is almost always recognisable, which is the clients dominant representational system and, furthermore, which Satir category might be characteristic.

However, what really counts is the effect of initiating subconscious processes by working through the questionnaire. This ensures that the client is well prepared when the actual session takes place and, thus, the maximum benefit can be achieved. For this reason, it is crucial that the time-span between answering the questionnaire and the Energetic-Hypnosis date ranges from at least two days to at most one week.

Similar purposes are often pursued by preliminary or initial interviews that build an imperative component of some therapeutic approaches. Although they do have the advantage of allowing the coach a more comprehensive impression of the personality of the client than a questionnaire ever could. There is, yet, the considerable risk of getting lost in trivialities and to miss out important aspects that the thorough study of a completed questionnaire would have revealed easily. Also, the additional scheduling effort usually is out of proportion to the potential benefits, which usually are not realized, anyway.

Besides the standardization and the ease of postal and digital transmission, the questionnaire technique also has the decisive advantage that the client can deal with the questions really intense and without feeling forced into a hasty reply like in a face to face dialogue situation. Only this guarantees the described positive effects.

So now let's take a look at the magical questions!

As an example, a questionnaire is given that is used specifically in the context of non-smoking coaching. The questions are in italics, followed by detailed explanations.

1. How intense is your motivation to become a non-smoker? (please mark on the scale)?

None..Very strong

The self-assessment of their own motivation will inevitably cause reasoning, how determined one is to achieve the alleged objectives. Often, this has not been considered sufficiently intense before. Of course, it is of crucial importance for the outcome that one's motivation is strong enough. Therefore, it is quite possible that with only very slight enthusiasm for the desired result (which is frequently so with 'visitors'), honesty at this point will exhibit that realistically no success can be expected and, therefore, the whole endeavour does not make much sense. This is perfectly legitimate and also saves money, effort and frustration. Empirical evidence shows that in such a case it is almost impossible to achieve the specified goal. Yet, this does not mean that this cannot change over time. Often, the internal processes need just a little while until the right moment is up. Then the chances of success are inclined substantially.

The mark on the scale offers important information to the coach with regard to what will be the priorities in the upcoming session and whether there is a requirement to support and strengthen the motivation by means of appropriate suggestions.

2. What is your motivation to become a non-smoker? What positive effects do you expect?

This raises the question about the intentions behind the goal. Consciously and subconsciously, this initiates the impulse to ditect, what the client would like to achieve beyond superficial announcements. Very often the declared purpose, non-smoking in this case, serves as a mere vehicle to realize some other, perhaps more important, goals. Or there might be a disguised purpose that the client does not admit to himself, for whatever reason. Although it is not likely that such motivations will be formulated as explicit answers, that does not matter. For the actual intention is, indeed, the triggering of subconscious processes as explained above.

Furthermore, the skilled eye of an experienced coach will generally be able to recognize what is going on, anyway. Often the things untold are more eloquent than the actual words.

3. What kept you from becoming a non-smoker, so far? What did you try?

This question's purpose is to inspire the client to look closely at the reasons of previous failure. Thus, it might provide new insights in how to deal with these obstacles and possibly remove them in the future.

The coach gets an overview, which approaches were not successful in the past and it may also offer an idea, to what extent distress and frustration exist. This is important in order to address the reasons for each failure individually.

4. What disadvantages might occur if you were a non-smoker? What would you have to deal with in that instance?

Now, the emphasis is directed towards the future. Almost certainly the desired achievement of the goal shall have negative consequences for the client as well. The plain fact that previous approaches were unsuccessful is a clear indicator that there are powerful subconscious reasons, which impede the achievement. By the mental association with the wanted state, they will be tracked down. Again, the same is true as with question 2 above that it is not important to have perfect answers already.

The nature and extent of the particular information provides valuable clues as to how pronounced and how accessible or inaccessible the subconscious obstacles are to the client.

5. What advantages did smoking offer? What of these aspects do you want to keep?

This sums up the previous questions in order to intensify the effect and to scrutinize the existing positive aspects of smoking. Secondly, it proves that it is the central approach of Energetic-Hypnosis to not take away anything dear, but, quite the opposite, that the areas that are important shall be maintained or even improved.

The answers display, what is essential for the client and where the values and needs are situated. This is extremely useful and helpful for the designing of the intervention.

6. What do you need to become a non-smoker? How much time this endeavour will afford?

The exploring of the useful and necessary tools has already led to an activation of conscious and/or subconscious searches for possible resources. The specification of the expected time frame for the desired change avoids counter-productive pressure and unrealistic expectations.

The comments allow the coach to plan and implement key steps for a successful change and to get an idea of how fast progress might be achievable. Taking into account, what the client does regard as feasible is crucial for lasting success.

63

Exercise: Questionnaire

1. Choose an issue or a goal of your own and rewrite the questionnaire in an adequate way.

2. Now, answer the questions in written form.

____

____

____

____

____

____

____

____

3. Write down the new insights about yourself that you gained already by now? What have you learned about your issue?

____

____

____

____

____

____

4. Wait three days and write down what changes with respect to your issue occurred and which additional insights you gained.

5. Ask at least two persons to name you an issue or a goal. It must not be a significant problem. Create an appropriate questionnaire for each one.

6. Ask them to answer the relevant questionnaire. What conclusions do you draw from the answers? In which way would you design an intervention, based on that information?

12. Transcript Energetic-Hypnosis-Session

Now you are going join a typical Energetic-Hypnosis coaching session. This ones purpose was to liberate the client from a cigarette addiction. In this particular case it was a 42-year-old male, who started to smoke cigarettes at the age of fifteen and continued to do so ever since. Currently, he is consuming about one and a half packets of cigarettes per day.

The left column displays the dialogue between hypnotist and client while in the right one you will find the detailed explanations of what is currently going on. You might get the most benefit out of the transcript if you initially cover the right half of each page and evaluate by yourself what is happening. I recommend that you act as thoroughly as possible, preferred in written form. Afterwards you may compare your own notes with the proposed remarks. This shall offer you the most significant success in gaining experience and knowledge.

H: displays verbal utterances of the hypnotist.

C: displays verbal utterances of the client.

(Italics in brackets) displays nonverbal activity.

H: Thank you very much for returning the questionnaire. You noted that your motivation is very high. That is excellent and offers the optimal foundation for success.	The client is acknowledged and encouraged in his behaviour and given the feedback that the intensity of his self-motivation offers a promising starting point. This represents both pacing and leading towards the proposed changes.
I ask you to please formulate the goal of our meeting again. In your own words, please.	The client is asked to formulate his own individual aims of the meeting. This marks explicitly, what is to be done, in contrast to what may be outside the range of the of the client's needs. Additionally, the formulation of the goal according to the well-formedness criteria is initiated.

C: Well, I want to quit smoking. I already tried several things. Chewing-gums with nicotine and also an interesting book. It worked for a few days but, sooner or later, I always started smoking again. I am aware that it is not healthy and costs a lot of money, too.

Often clients formulate a quite vague target at first and start to distract the conversation from the issue.

H: That is the crucial point. The reasons to quit smoking are all well known. Still, only few people are able to get rid of the cigarettes for good. In my experience, the physical addiction is massively overrated. Withdrawal symptoms occur seldom and after three or four days the nicotine has completely left the body. It is mainly a matter of the mind. Yet it is important to realise that smoking indeed serves some positive intentions. If you simply take it away, you leave a gap that craves to be filled again.

The hypnotist uses the opportunity and addresses the client's comments to prepare the subsequent intervention and to offer the client some new perspectives and views.

C: I never looked at it that way.

The answer confirms the success of the intention.

H: It is often possible to keep hands off cigarettes quite a while with self-imposed effort. Nevertheless they often remain permanently on one's mind. Thus, this will work until some stressful situation, or a night out with a bit of alcohol, comes along. Very often, one may start smoking again in such an instance.

Describing experiences that many smokers are familiar with mirrors their view and therefore shall intensify the rapport. The use of 'one' is done intentionally. This allows the client to pick these aspect that meet his situation, while he can skip those that are unknown to him, without any probably negative effect on the rapport.

C: Yeah, I experienced things like that.

The answer confirms the success of the intention.

H: Many people fill the resulting gap with sweets, for example. That's quite a similar oral procedure. Of course, one might gain weight rapidly because of that. Still, this is only a vicarious satisfaction which cannot really replace the cigarettes.

Thus, I kindly ask you again to define the aim of our meeting precisely.

C: I want to be a non-smoker.

H: At what date do you want to have reached this?

C: Mmh, maybe right now? Is this possible?

H: Well, people differ. Some of my clients walk out of the door and never touch a cigarette again. I even experienced some cases, when the person couldn't even remember that they ever smoked at all. Others take a few days until the progress has integrated into their personality and the urge to smoke disappears bit by bit. This is mainly due to the structure of your subconscious.

We shall address this in detail in the course of the trance. Do you have any experiences with hypnosis?

Once again, describing the experiences that many smokers are familiar with, mirrors their view of the world and therefore shall intensify the rapport.

Now, that the comments of the client have been addressed extensively, he is asked to define his goal more precise than before.

The answer isn't much more precise, anyway.

Thus, the hypnotist starts to ask more precise questions.

The time frame is fixed.

The hypnotist defines the range of possible outcomes. The eventual success is presupposed in any case.

It is important, as well for the preparation as much as for the subsequent induction, to know whether the client already has any experiences with hypnosis. Or what his ideas about it are, respectively.

C: I do not have any own experiences. I am curious but also a bit anxious.

If the client already had some experiences, it was best to refer to that. Otherwise, as in this case it is recommended to offer some general information on the subject and to list some similar experiences that are well-known to the client.

On the tube there was a hypnosis-show recently. That was very impressive.

If the ideas about hypnosis are mainly influenced by stage-hypnotism, it is very important to address this and to clarify that this is something completely different.

H: Yes, that certainly is. However, stage-hypnotism is something absolutely different. The trance state, we are about to work with instead, is something that you are very familiar with. You experience this every night, right before you fall asleep. This pleasant and tender feeling of relaxation when you are still aware of everything that surrounds you and, yet, the environment recedes more and more while you start to focus on your inner processes and perceptions. Every now and then, you may slide a bit into dreaming and enjoy letting go more and more.

The client is offered the state right before falling asleep as reference. This is done slowly and in detail because the client starts to recall this condition and that will inevitably make him slip into a light trance already. This is supported by the fact that virtually everyone experiences the described condition as very pleasant.

C: Ah yeaaaah, that is very fine.

The answer confirms the success of the intention.

<u>H:</u> I'd like to tell you now, what we are about to do in the next hour. First, I will guide you into a light trance which enables us to get easy access to your subconscious mind. Next, we will disclose the highest positive intention that smoking meant to you. This is often found in regions that you would never ever have thought or dreamed of. The good thing is that you do not have to give me any information on what that might be. Subsequently, we shall find alternative ways to fulfil this purpose in a far better manner than smoking could ever have accomplished.

The hypnotist explains in detail the process of the now following intervention. On the one hand, this causes increased confidence in the action because the client gains an insight into what to expect and, on the other hand, it directs his thoughts towards a supporting route.

Since it is best for the state of trance if you do not talk, we shall communicate by means of so-called finger signals. I.e. you or your subconscious mind shows a yes-signal with the index finger of one hand whenever I ask you a question, which you want to answer by 'yes'. Which hand would you prefer for this purpose?

This question regarding a basically insignificant decision is made decisively after the stream of new information. Important to note is the subtle suggestion that the subconscious mind will cause the finger signals.

C: Ähhh, mmh, ähh, the right one. For I am right-handed.

This will regularly provoke a slight confusion and afford explicit reorientation on behalf of the client to be able to give a reply. This causes the former information to sink into the subconscious. That is quite helpful with regard to the upcoming interventions. Especially, it prevents the not very fruitful discussions on certain points which arise, most likely, more as a kind of avoidance behaviour than out of a real need for information. Very fascinating is the pseudo-rationalization of the choice for the right hand. The human mind seems to be designed to need a logical reasoning for every decision.

H: Great! And with the index finger of the left hand you shall signal a 'No'.

The assignment of the signals is reinforced.

As soon as this is accomplished, and you were able to get all kinds of experience and some confidence in the state of hypnotic trance, we will deepen this further.

At this point, the presupposition is now introduced that the experiences gained by then will have led to confidence in the hypnotic state and, further more, that this offers a perfect basis for a deepening of the trance.

For that purpose I will touch your shoulder and your wrist. Is that okay?

The permission for physical contact is obtained. On the one hand, to see if the client has any objections against such a contact and, on the other, to prepare him for this very touching. Thus, this shall not cause any unpleasant surprise that might interfere negatively with the trance. Moreover, the announcement stated in that way will, in fact, even reinforce

<u>**C:**</u> Yes, that is okay.

<u>**H:**</u> Do you have any further questions?

<u>**C:**</u> No, none at all.

<u>**H:**</u> Great! Now let's start with a little experiment. Interlace the fingers of your two hands. Now stretch your two index fingers and hold them apart. As you try to keep them separated, your subconscious mind will make them approach each other more and more ... like through a magnetic force they are pulled towards each other ... more and more ... until they eventually touch each other and stick like glue.

<u>**C:**</u> I'm impressed!

<u>**H:**</u> Okay, now sit back comfortably and, please, put your hands on your thighs. Pay attention to the things that you can still perceive here in the room. Perhaps, you can hear the ticking of the clock on the wall and, possibly, the feeling of chair you sit on. And while you may recognize the structure of the door of the wardrobe in front of you, you may have noticed that your breathing has already changed a bit and your body has relaxed a little bit more.

the trance later on, as soon as the contact takes place.

The client agrees.

Once again, especially to enforce the rapport, the client is explicitly offered the opportunity to ask questions.

This suggestibility test, also named 'Convincer', takes the client into a light trance state and, additionally, demonstrates the strength and power of his subconscious. Furthermore, it provides valuable clues about the degree of suggestibility of the client. This offers some inference about the kind and duration of the induction and the type of suggestions that have to be granted during the trance.

The induction starts with the typical directing of the attention towards three perceptions in the external environment, in this case, the ticking of the clock (auditory), feeling of the chair (kinaesthetic) and structure of the wardrobe door (visually), followed by two internal perceptions (modified breathing, more relaxed body). This is done in the vague Ericksonian style (perhaps, possibly, may) and the indirectly given suggestions of relaxation and changes in behaviour, which can not be refuted easily by the client in this

And as my voice will accompany your subconscious mind anywhere in the next hour, your conscious mind does not have to listen any longer.

You may also listen to the music and, perhaps, you might have noticed that your eyelids feel a little heavier with every blink until it is simply more comfortable to let them remain closed.

(The client closes his eyes)

Great!

And I'm going to ask you to open your eyes briefly but only as I say, "Now!".

As soon as you shall close them again, you will notice that the relaxation in your body has become much more intense.

situation. Since the test with the convincer has proven that the client is an excellent trance subject, the 3-2-1 structure is slightly abbreviated.

Conscious and subconscious attention of the client are directed towards different directions. And the conscious mind is asked to no longer pay attention to what is being said.

Once again the attention is guided from external (music) to internal perceptions (heaviness of the eyelids), still artfully vague ("You may ... perhaps, you might ...") but, this time, with clearer and somewhat more direct suggestions to control the behaviour of the client and to make him close his eyes.

The suggestions proves to be successful.

The client's behaviour is confirmed. This promotes the rapport and encourages the acceptance of other suggestions.

Because the client was very susceptible to the previous suggestion of eye closure, this can be used as a starting signal to leave the permissive induction style and, instead, use the Elman methodology.

Again, the desired physical response of opening and closing the eyes is causally linked to the suggestion of an even intensified relaxation.

Now!

(The client opens his eyes. The hypnotist holds his index and middle finger about 12 inches in front of the client, slightly above his eyes)

Look at my fingers!

(Client stares at the fingers of the coach who moves them quickly downwards in front of the face and the body of the client. Client closes his eyes again and exhales)

Excellent! And since you may have noticed that the relaxation in your body has increased, we now do it all over again. And you will be able to even double your relaxation.

Now!

(The whole procedure is repeated. The client displays severe difficulties to open his eyes again)

The suggestions proves to be successful.

Now the order is given explicitly.

The eye-closure in combination with the exhaling indicates the effectiveness of the suggestion.

Because of the obvious success, the client's reaction is positively confirmed and reaffirmed. This is used as a new causality, which assumes that a further repetition of the procedure will even increase the effect.

The hesitation in re-opening the eyes is a very good indicator of the depth of the altered state that the client has reached in the meantime. The result of this temporary opening of the eyes is a slight getting out of the hypnotic state with a subsequent return into it. This is a fractionation of the trance. The effect is a progressively deeper trance state each time, as the reaction of the client demonstrates.

And as you have noticed, it is now much more comfortable to keep your eyes closed and extend this pleasant feeling of heaviness from the eyelids to your entire body. Exactly.

And now, as you can experience your body in a completely relaxed state, you will also be able to relax and free your mind.

As I count backwards from ten to zero, your mind will relax more and more with every number.

Ten - Nine - please watch your thoughts come and pass by - Eight - Seven - Six - Five, and it feels better and better - Four - and with no doubt you have now reached a very free and pleasant state - Two - One - Zero

And it might get even lower, Minus One - Minus Two - Minus Three.

The client's reaction is used and utilised to extend the feeling of heaviness of the eyelids to the rest of the body, by the use of a simple conjunction ('and').

By means of a causal conjunction ('as') the obvious physical relaxation is transmitted to the mind of the client.

Predetermined in this way, the client is now announced, what will take place next and, again, with the help of a simple conjunction ('and'), he is presented the suggestion that the counting will cause the relaxation of his mind.

The slow and quiet counting, in which some suggestions are integrated, reinforces the intended effect. Number three is phonetically 'hidden' (free) to confuse and disorientate the conscious mind while the subconscious is very well able to recognise structures like that and is readily willing to accept the attached suggestions.

In a similar way the previously unannounced, yet of course, logical continuation of counting into the numbers of the negative realm leads to surprise and confusion, which will result in a further intensification of the suggested relaxation.

Because your mind is now completely open, the time has come that I turn to the part of your personality that has had the responsibility for smoking so far.

The Six-Step-Reframing starts with contacting the part that is responsible for smoking.

(The hypnotist changes his position now and speaks to the client from an altered direction)

This change in the direction of speaking implies an analogue marking which stresses, that from now on the communication takes place with a different aspect of the client's personality.

I honour explicitly everything that you previously did for C and tried to achieve for him. I know that you always pursued absolutely positive intentions. And as soon as you're ready to communicate with us, I ask you to indicate that to me with the right index finger.

The part of the personality is now fully respected and explicitly confirmed in order to establish excellent rapport with it. Then, his willingness to communicate is requested. The term 'as soon as' implies that this willingness exists, only the time period for a response is left undetermined (this is the key difference and advantage to the word 'if'!)

(After a while, the right index finger of the client moves cautiously)

Contact is established.

I thank you most sincerely for the fact that you are willing to communicate with us. I ask you to tell C the positive intention that you wanted to achieve for him with the cigarettes, so far. And once you have communicated this to him, please indicate this to me with the right index finger.
(After a while, the right index finger of the client moves cautiously)

The response is appreciated and the second step is initiated by requesting the positive intention.

Thank you! And if you now look a little bit further, there may even be another purpose hidden behind. Is that right?

(After a while, the right index finger of the client moves cautiously)

Very good! Please let him know this one as well and, then, signal this to me with your right index finger.

(After a while, the right index finger of the client moves cautiously)

Thank you! If you now look a little bit further, there may even be another purpose hidden behind. Is that right?

(After a while, the left index finger of the client moves cautiously)

No! Now, we have found the highest positive intention that you were trying to achieve in the past by smoking. Did you really achieve this goal by means of smoking?

(After a while, the left index finger of the client moves cautiously)

No, not really! Would it be in your interest to get some new alternatives that might realise that purpose in a much better way than smoking did?

Now, the third step takes place in order to disclose the highest positive intention. Since C is a kinaesthetic person, his subconscious is accessed by using visual terminology.

Question is answered with 'Yes!'.

The former procedure is repeated.

Again, the former procedure is repeated.

Question is answered with 'no'. This implies that the highest positive intention has been disclosed.

The link between the highest positive intention and the previous behaviour is challenged.

Question is answered with 'No!'.

Consent for the search for new options is obtained.

(After a while, the right index finger of the client moves cautiously)

Question is answered with 'Yes!'.

Very good! For now, I thank you for your kind cooperation and turn to the part of your personality, which includes all of your creativity.

The part is again explicitly acknowledged. Subsequently, the transition to the fourth step of the process is initiated.

(The hypnotist changes his position once again and speaks to the client from an altered direction)

This change in the direction of speaking implies an analogue marking, underlining that now the communication takes place with a different aspect of the client's personality.

As soon as the creative part is ready to communicate with us, it shall signal this with the right index finger.

The creative part's willingness to communicate is requested.

(After a while, the right index finger of the client moves cautiously)

Contact is established.

Thank you very much! Now, you know already, what I want to ask of you, as you were able to watch, what was going on before. Therefore, please create five new alternatives that meet the positive intention of the other part far better than smoking. Every time you found a new variant, please, indicate this by means of moving the right index finger in the familiar way.

The creative part is asked to create five alternatives and indicate this each time.

(Successively, the right index finger of the clients moves five times)

Client shows the desired response.

Thank you! I now turn to the original part that was formerly responsible for smoking.

(The hypnotist changes his position back to the one he had when he was talking to the first part of the client's personality for the first time)

So, now you can see the five alternatives, which were developed by the creative part. I ask you whether each of them is a new option that you like and want to implement as new behaviour from now on.

(The hypnotist addresses each of the five variants individually. In this case, the client displays a 'no'-signal with the second proposal by moving the left index finger. Thus, this one is simply skipped)

Thank you! So, from now on you posses four new alternatives that are qualified to fulfil your most positive intention far better than smoking used to.

(The hypnotist returns to the neutral position)

Communication with the creative part is completed. Now, the hypnotist addresses the first part again.

This change in the direction of speaking implies an analogue marking, additionally indicating that now the communication takes place with the original aspect of the client's personality.

The part is asked to review and approve for each of the five new alternatives.

Thy query reveals that all but the second proposal are accepted.

This result is summarized and reinforced.

Since there are now four new options, which even exceeds the required minimum number of three alternatives, step four is completed (at least for the moment).

So, now the time has come to ask if there are any other parts of your personality that might have any reservations regarding the four new alternatives?

(After a while, the left index finger of the client moves cautiously)

That is great! Now, everything is perfect for the realization of the new alternatives and the achievement of your goal.

Therefore, I ask you now to put yourself mentally one month ahead into the future. To a point in time, when you have already reached your goal to be smoke-free. Feel intensively how pleasant it is to have achieved this goal and how nice it is to have experienced your new opportunities for a few weeks now. Look around, what you can see there and listen, what there is to be heard as well

Thus, the fifth step follows: the Eco-Check. It is supposed to clarify whether the new options are not only in the interest of the former smoking part but, also, in line with the overall personality of the client.

Question is answered with 'No!'. Hence, there are no obvious reservations by other aspects of the client's personality.

This result is also reflected and reinforced.

Now, the final stage of the Six-Step-Reframing can be carried out. The client is taken into the future mentally to a time, when his goal is already achieved. He gets the advice to experience this with intense association. The three main sensory channels VAK are explicitly addressed in order to draw the attention fully to a complete sensory experience.

At this point, the classical scheme is completed. The process of Energetic-Hypnosis, however, goes some important steps beyond. Because the traditional Six-Step-Reframing misses several essential energetic aspects, which have proven to stabilise the success substantially and eliminate the need for the otherwise often required follow-up appointments.

And once you have enjoyed this state extensively enough, I ask you to float out of yourself and take some sort of an eagle's perspective and look down on C, who has reached his goal. Consider whether he requires any abilities or resources in order to be able to reach his goal even more perfect. Is there anything?

(After a while, the right index finger of the client moves cautiously)

Yes, there's still something missing. Therefore, I ask you now to float back through time, like over a line that represents your life, bit by bit, year after year, step by step, up to a memory or an experience, when this ability was at your disposal. And once you've found it, show it to me again with your right index finger.

(After a while, the right index finger of the client moves cautiously)

Great! And now make this experience a little bit more intense. Feel in every cell of your body how pleasant it is to have this ability. And then, you make it even stronger once more.

And as soon as it is just right for you, take it with you, back to the future and insert it in your goal.

The client is now dissociated from himself and the situation. From this perspective, it is considerably easier to assess, which additional resources should be added or what could guarantee the achievement of the goal.

Question is answered with 'Yes!'.

Client is asked to go backwards through time to some point in the past, where he used to possess the desired resource.

Question is answered with 'Yes!'. This indicates that the client found it.

Suggestions are offered to associate the client with the experience and to make the perception of this resource as vivid as possible in order to reinforce it.

The client is re-associated to the target situation and the new resource is added to it.

And now, as your goal has been enriched even further, pay attention to what aspects feel even better now.

And once you have enjoyed this even more intense now, return to the eagle's view and watch C down there. Is there anything else necessary for him?.

(After a while, the left index finger of the client moves cautiously)

No! Now everything is complete, everything is perfect. And, therefore, I ask you now to float back down, return into your body and enjoy, once again, the perfect achievement of your goal.

And, now, you look back to the past when the present was the future and the past was the present and, finally, you return to today.

And from the present, please, perform in your mind the first important step towards your future goal. Look forward to all the small and large steps and all the exciting changes that are waiting for you on the way there.

The client's attention is explicitly directed to the changes that occurred. They should be declared as improvements, anyway, to intensify the experience and awareness of the progress.

After a further suggestion, which increases the anticipation of the experience of the realized goal once more, the client is dissociated again to look for other necessary or useful items.

Question is answered with 'No!'.

Therefore, the client is brought back from dissociation into association.

Playing with the temporary references exhibits a disorientational effect that is intended to confuse the timing of the achievements and, thus, transfer it to the present day immediately.

And, once again, the future events are charged with pleasant emotions to ensure the transfer of the results.

Now, I will touch your right shoulder as I had told you before.

(The hypnotist places his left hand on the client's right shoulder)

Very gently, with every slight pressure of my hand, you will slide deeper and deeper into this pleasant state of hypnosis, deeper and deeper.

(The hypnotist presses repeatedly the client's shoulder, tender but noticeable)

And while you slip deeper and deeper, I will grab your right wrist and raise your arm.

(The hypnotist grabs with his right hand the client's right wrist and ralses the arm gently)

The following contact is announced. This is important to avoid any potential negative interference of the physical contact. Additionally, it activates the preliminary suggestion that this would be done in connection with a deepening of the trance. Thus, the announcement shall convey a respective expectation.

Physical contact is established.

Explicit suggestion and announcements are granted in order to intensify the trance state.

The announcement is carried out. Especially in the current phase, the verification of announcements results in a strengthening of the rapport and in an increased willingness to obey the following suggestions.

The next activity is announced.

The announcement is carried out.

Just let your arm remain hanging in the air and concentrate your attention now on your right index finger. All good feelings that you have ever felt in your life are now gathered in it, as well as all the energy that you have ever wanted. And the good feelings and the energy want to become stronger, and the good feelings and the energy long to expand out of your finger, first, into the hand and, from there on, into the arm and, from there on, further into every fibre of your body. Yeah, exactly that way.

And I can now let go of your shoulder and you can, thus, sink even deeper into trance. And your arm will remain in the air and will descend exactly as fast as all the changes are fully integrated into your personality and everything is now perfectly restructured. And, meanwhile, I shall remain silent, for your subconscious may carry out the task completely undisturbed.

(The hypnotist remains silent while the arm of the client descents gradually until the right hand comes to a rest on the thighs)

The attention of the client is guided to his right index finger. It is, of course, not a coincidence that this is the finger, which had been previously associated with a positive 'yes' attitude. Suggestions are given regarding good feelings and energy. The statements are kept very general in order to offer the client maximum freedom to insert his personal experiences and preferences at this point.

Since all changes and goals have been installed, the client gets the opportunity to internalise all of that without any disturbances. The movement of the arm indicates, how far this process has progressed and when the integration is implemented.

The order regarding the levitation of the arm is carried out.

Very good! And now, I'll give you 10 minutes to complete all the energetic adjustments that allow you, from now on, to achieve this and many other goals in a perfect way and at the perfect rate. I will bang a gong. Let yourself be carried away by the pleasant sound and when I shall bang the gong again, after 10 minutes, you will have activated all energetic resources.

(The hypnotist hits the gong. As soon as the sound has slowly faded away, he waits about 20 seconds(!) and hits it again)

Now, your subconscious has learned in a pleasant way all the things it takes to be able to realise this and many other goals from now on.

A central concern of Energetic-Hypnosis is to act on a generalised level. This means to not just get a grip on the current topic but to convey generalised learning experiences that reach far beyond. The client and, even more so, his subconscious shall be enabled to address any other issues in new ways. This is called 'Deutero-Learning' in the sense of Gregory Bateson.

The announcement is apparently implemented. However, instead of the advertised 10 minutes, only 20 seconds pass between the two gongs. In the deep trance state, in which the client is now, this discrepancy, which is never registered by a client, induces a strong time distortion in order to exhibit dramatically beneficial effects upon the internal processing, anchoring and realization of all the given energetic learning suggestions. Unfortunately, the benefits of this impressive outcomes are utilized by hardly any hypnotist. The use of an acoustic signal to mark the beginning and end, as in this example a gong, supports the mental separation of this very special process from the rest of the action.

The experience just made is confirmed and enforced verbally, once again.

And you know your subconscious works best the less your conscious mind knows about it and the less it interferes with it. Hence, it is probably a good idea to forget everything your consciousness does not need to know because your subconscious mind knows everything it needs to know. So, you can forget everything we have done, like in a the way a dream does fade away. One moment ago, you knew that you had one but, now, you are able to grasp less and less of what you had actually dreamed about. And, yet, you had that dream and, thus, its effects become even stronger.

Slowly, very slowly, the time has come to return fully into the here and now. For a little while, enjoy the pleasant relaxed state a little bit more. I'm going to count from one to ten slowly, and with each number you get to perceive a little bit more of the environment. But only when I reach the number ten, you will open your eyes again and feel wonderfully recovered, like after a refreshing nap.

One - Two - Three - now you hear my voice loud and clear - Four - Five – and you feel the chair on which you sit - Six - and now you hear the music in the background - Seven - and even register again the light that shines through your eyelids - Eight - Nine - and now you open your eyes again - Ten - stretch, look around, take a deep breath!

Amnesia is suggested to forget most of the events of the preceding hypnosis session. This is also done in a very vague manner, for it is left to the subconscious of the client, which parts it might make accessible to the conscious memory and which not. Overall, it is quite advantageous that only very little is still available to conscious memory because, otherwise, this might affect the initiated processes negatively.

The client is now prepared for the extro in a gentle way. It is emphasised that he should feel well and recovered afterwards. This also facilitates the willingness to return from the very pleasant trance back into the waking state. Adequate suggestions are presented.

Now the extro with the gradual reorientation to the 'here and now' is performed.

Maybe you want to drink some water?

(Client and hypnotist drink a few sips of water from their glasses)

How do you feel about smoking now? What changes do you experience?

The perceived changes are inquired. Thus, the attention of the client is distracted from the previous hypnotic process in order to promote and accelerate amnesia. In addition, he should immediately become aware of the achieved progress.

C: Hmm, I do not know. Anyway, I currently do not fancy a cigarette.

Obviously, the intervention was successful ☺

13. Final Remark

Throughout this book, you have learned many things about Energetic-Hypnosis, about your subconscious mind and about yourself. You have done numerous exercises and worked through the transcript. Therefore, you deserve a reward, a little energetic story.

Of course, it is designed to offer you lots of enrichment and inspiration, too. Hence, a bit of advice. Look for a quiet corner, take about 20 minutes of time, relax and read through the story as a whole, at once. This ensures the maximum effect. Recommended is to read it right before bedtime.

I wish you sweet and informative dreams!

Best regards

Dr. Claus Wunderlich

14. Epilogue: The Sun and the Family Book

When the evening comes, the sun descents towards the horizon more and more and it slides deeper and deeper down, heavy and tired from the day's experiences and, finally, little by little, piece by piece, sinks behind it. Dusk begins with a blink until, eventually, the night closes in. The sun is now roaming somewhere else, far away. It sleeps and dreams, softly and relaxed, and does not know what is going on during its absence. But, of course, a lot happens in the dark. Many things are changing and some will disappear, even very, very old ones. And entirely new ones shall arise while some things take on a completely different shape.

It was often with those sunsets that we played hide and seek as kids. Right at the time when a warm, relaxed atmosphere laid on the landscape. You know certainly, how to play it? One covers both eyes and counts slowly backwards: 10 - 9 - 8 - 7 - 6 - 5 - 4 - 3 – 2 - 1! Meanwhile, the others hide somewhere. The better one does it the harder one is to be found. And so, it often took a long span of time until finally each one was found. I remember, once, when I was the one who had to search the others, there was a girl that I could not find at all. Although I had discovered all the others for quite a while already. I searched everywhere that I could guess. She might hide behind trees, in bushes, in an old barn, under a ton, even under parked cars, everywhere. She wasn't there. I began to worry, after all, it was really dark now. Meanwhile, the others helped in the search for her hiding place. We yelled and ran around, getting more and more nervous and even started to panic. It took some time until eventually one declared that we had searched everywhere that she could be. Probably, she was making a joke and had gone home. That sounded quite pursuant because we knew her and had made similar experiences with her already, more than once.

After all, she was a member of a very unusual family. A very, very old family. In this family, there was something really special. It was an ancient and heavy book, which for many, many centuries was owned by the family and was passed on from one generation to the next. Since it was that old and everyone had dealt extensively with it, because it was very pleasant to read in it, the pages were massively yellowed. Although the envelope had been renewed from time to time, it usually did not last for very long before it looked worn again.

The language of the book was mainly a little antiquated and awkward but every generation and each family member was always able to exactly understand, what was written and what was meant. Even though some things did not seem to make much sense. Especially appealing were the many beautiful images that covered part of some pages and sometimes even decorated an entire page. Many were painted with indescribably beautiful colours that had not bleached over the centuries and decades. There were also drawings that were only in black and white and some even looked just like sketches that were never completed. It was difficult to tell whether the images all came from the same painter and nobody could ever find out. Nor will the question ever be answered whether the texts stem from different authors. Somehow, that wasn't very interesting, anyway.

More important had always been that the advice given was strictly obeyed. And that was passed from parents to children and from grandparents to grandchildren and from one to another. Some things did seem odd and, perhaps, not at all adequate but certainly everything had its meaning and purpose. And if one does not quite understand it, then, maybe, because the person is too young or not smart enough. Finally, the book and what it tells is so much older and has served very well in the past, didn't it? Otherwise it would not have been passed on and on from one to another, right?

Yet, over the years and decades and centuries that passed, it happened more frequently that things did not fit that perfectly any longer. And also did not really work the way they used to. Yes, often members of the family found themselves very unhappy, sad with their lives, without knowing quite what could be the reason. All had worked out so well for their parents and grandparents by what the book had advised and told. Of course, not everything has always been completely perfect. Who would expect that? But, actually, they had coped with themselves and the world very well? Even though the circumstances certainly had been much more difficult in the past.

Eventually, the girl that we know from the hide and seek game, was handed the book, later, when she had grown up. She has always been a little different from the rest of the family. No wonder, thus, that she also received much well-meant advice and words of warning. Of course, she had always known the importance of the book and she was very happy and excited to hold it in her hands now. She was very curious and could not await to read it from the first page to the final one. And she was amazed, how much it had to offer to her and how beautiful it was and in how many ways it was able to enrich her knowledge and her live. And so it received a very special place in her apartment and, whenever she could, she read in it and earned valuable advice from those old stories of her family that had lost none of their meaning and wisdom over all that time. Especially at moments, when she was not feeling that fine, when she was sad and even a little desperate, it was an indescribable fountainhead of comfort and full of invaluable hints on how to return on the right track.

One night, many years later, at a time, when everything seemed to follow a steady course, when she had established her live quite well, and the days came and went in a way that she was used to for a long time, she had an unusual dream. Normally, she did not dream often, only sometimes. Most of the times, she could remember a bit of a dreams after waking but soon the pictures faded gradually, like sand running through your fingers, until finally nothing remained in her memory. Who knows how many times she has had this dream before without being able to remember? Or, perhaps, the time had not yet been ripe. Because this time, everything was different. In the middle of the night, she woke out of the dream, was wide awake at once and aware of things with a clarity, which otherwise may only be experienced by enlightened individuals. It was clearly visible that this dull, subliminal sadness and melancholy that has spread through her days more and more and almost unnoticed, this vague feeling of unhappiness and futility which she had always tried to banish from her live and her feelings one way or another, however, with less and less success, all of that did not exist despite the book but, actually, because of the book!

That very instant changed her whole view and perspective. Like in a rush, she got up and flipped through the book from front to back. Granted, there was much truth and good inside but she now realized very clearly that a lot of things written in it were total bullshit and nonsense. Somehow, she suddenly could not understand any more why she and her ancestors always had regarded each letter as kind of a holy truth. And she wondered why it was her to discover how much rubbish she and the others had believed and obeyed for such a long time. Was it her subconscious, which, for some unknown reason, understood more? Or was it perhaps because she has always been a bit, as they say, over the rainbow? Many times she had tried new and unusual things and ways. For she was actually pretty smart and has always been.

After all, it is not important, what the reasons might have been, anyway. And she didn't mind at all since she was just too happy that she had opened her eyes eventually. With renewed energy, she did something that no member of her family would ever have dared before. She tore out all the pages that were simply too stupid. She left some chapters in it, yet, laughed very heartily at what was written there. And, of course, there were a few things, even many, she still considered as very useful and helpful. She realised that some texts must have been very reasonable at the time when they were written but have become obsolete in the meantime. Others have always been pure idiocy. Now she was quite sure about that. And some are still valuable. Whether this may still be true tomorrow? Only time will tell.

She came to the conclusion that now was the time to put this old book in the closet. There it had its place, because she wanted to remember it and maybe take a look inside, every now and then. So it was good to know that it is there and that the meaning has changed from now on thoroughly. And she also thought that she should write her own book which should include everything that is important and dear to her. It would become a very good book, for sure.

And she did not forget to write on the very first page in capital letters: you can, may and shall, at any time, write entirely new and completely different things inside this book, whenever you think or feel, the time has come. And you can cross out every word and every sentence if it does not fit any more. You may even tear out whole pages if you feel like doing this. And who knows, maybe eventually, the day might come, where I want to throw away the whole book to be happy. Perhaps, this will be the moment to write an entirely new book or, maybe, I won't need one at all any more. Who knows?

Most likely, it actually took an extraordinary person like her to do something courageous and determined like that. No wonder that it was her to enjoy hiding so well that no one could find her. It was the next morning, very early, that she appeared again. She never told anybody, where she had hidden all the time, so I do not know it, either. But she told the others, not without a good dose of triumph in her voice, "I was near, all of the time, and watched you. It has given me immense pleasure to observe how you looked for me. But I wanted to determine when you shall see me again!". Yes, that was the way that we always knew her, a bit self-willed, very clever and incredibly smart. We were pleased that she was now a part of us again, for she was anyway, even if she was out of sight for a while. Once the time is right, everything reappears.

Just the way the morning sun reappears. First, with a pale twilight, which becomes gradually brighter until finally the first narrow strip of the luminous disk blinks over the horizon again. And, bit by bit, it rises more and more above it and, finally, shines in full beauty down from the sky, which it had left the evening before. And it now appears that many things are no longer the way that they used to be the day before. Some things have changed very thoroughly during the time when it was elsewhere. But it is not of much interest, how and why and what might have happened because it is obvious that the result is perfect. And shall be so in the future, too.

And thus, the sun no longer thinks about, what has changed in its absence but notices occasionally, now and in the days to come, at one point or another, in one way or some other, everything that has become better than it used to be. And the sun enjoys it and is very grateful that it can trust that, even in its absence, great work can be done.

15. Bibliography

Bandler, Richard und Grinder, John (2005), Reframing. Ein ökologischer Ansatz in der Psychotherapie (NLP), 8. Auflage;
Junfermann Verlag, Paderborn

Bandler, Richard (1990), Veränderung des subjektiven Erlebens, Fortgeschrittene Methoden des NLP, 3. Auflage;
Junfermannsche Verlagsbuchhandlung, Paderborn

Bandler, Richard und Grinder, John (1985), Neue Wege der Kurzzeittherapie, Neurolinguistische Programme, 4. Auflage;
Junfermannsche Verlagsbuchhandlung, Paderborn

Bandler, Richard und Grinder, John (1991), Metasprache und Psychotherapie, Die Struktur der Magie II, 5. Auflage;
Junfermannsche Verlagsbuchhandlung, Paderborn

Bandler, Richard und Grinder, John (2001), Metasprache und Psychotherapie, Die Struktur der Magie I, 10. Auflage;
Junfermann Verlag, Paderborn

Bateson, Gregory (1985), Ökologie des Geistes: Anthropologische, psychologische, biologische und epistemologische Perspektiven, 10. Auflage;
Suhrkamp Verlag, Berlin

Berne, Eric (1983), Was sagen Sie, nachdem Sie Guten Tag gesagt haben?: Psychologie des menschlichen Verhaltens, 21. Auflage;
Fischer (Tb.), Frankfurt

Bodian, Stephan (2006), Meditation für Dummies: Wirken Sie mit Meditation dem Alltagsstress entgegen und steigern Sie ihr Wohlbefinden, 2. Auflage;
Wiley-VCH Verlag, Weinheim

Byrne, Rhonda (2007), The Secret - Das Geheimnis, 17. Auflage;
Arkana Verlag, Götting

Cooper, Linn und Erickson, Milton (2004), Time Distortion in Hypnosis, An Experimental and Clinical Investigation;
OTC Publishing Corp., Boca Raton FL

Derra, Claus (2007), Progressive Relaxation: Grundlagen und praktische Durchführung für Ärzte und Therapeuten;
Deutscher Arzte-Verlag, Köln

Ekman, Paul und Friese, Wallace (2003), Unmasking the Face, A Guide to Recognizing Emotions from Facial Expressions; Malor Books, Cambridge MA

Elman, Dave (1984), Hypnotherapy, New Edition;
Westwood Publishing Co, US

Erickson, Milton und Rossi, Ernest (2007a), Hypnose erleben. Veränderte Bewusstseinszustände therapeutisch nutzen;
J. G. Cotta'sche Buchhandlung Nachfolger GmbH, Stuttgart

Erickson, Milton und Rossi, Ernest (2007b), Hypnotherapie. Aufbau, Beispiele, Forschungen, 9. Auflage;
J. G. Cotta'sche Buchhandlung Nachfolger GmbH, Stuttgart

Erickson, Milton und Rossi, Ernest und Rossi, Sheila (2009), Hypnose: Induktion. Psychotherapeutische Anwendung. Beispiele. 7. Auflage;
J. G. Cotta'sche Buchhandlung Nachfolger GmbH, Stuttgart

Gordon, David (2005), Therapeutische Metaphern, 6. Auflage;
Junfermann Verlag, Paderborn

Grinder, John und Bandler Richard (2006), Therapie in Trance, Neurolinguistisches Programmieren (NLP) und die Struktur hypnotischer Kommunikation, 12. Auflage;
J. G. Cotta'sche Buchhandlung Nachfolger GmbH, Stuttgart

Grinder, John und Deloizer, Judith und Bandler, Richard (1996), Patterns of the Hypnotic Techniques of Milton H. Erickson, M.D. Volume II;
Grinder & Associates, Scotts Valley CA

Havener, Thorsten und Spitzbart, Michael (2010), Denken Sie nicht an einen blauen Elefanten!: Die Macht der Gedanken, 9. Auflage;
rororo Verlag, Reinbek

Hicks, Esther und Hicks, Jerry (2008), Wünschen und bekommen: Wie Sie Ihre Sehnsüchte erfüllen;
Ullstein Taschenbuchverlag, Berlin

James, Tad und Flores, Lorraine und Schober, Jack (2007), Kompaktkurs Hypnose: Wie man Phänomene tiefer Trance hervorruft. Ein umfassender Leitfaden, 2. Auflage;
Junfermann Verlag, Paderborn

Kossak, Hans-Christian (2004), Hypnose. Mit Audio-CD: Ein Lehrbuch für Psychotherapeuten und Ärzte, 4. vollst. überarb. Auflage;
Beltz Psychologie Verlags Union, Weinheim

Meier, Dave (2000), The Accelerated Learning Handbook: A Creative Guide to Designing and Delivering Faster, More Effective Training Programs;
Mcgraw-Hill Professional

Mohl, Alexa (2007), Das Metaphern-Lernbuch: Geschichten und Anleitungen aus der Zauberwerkstatt, 5. Auflage;
Junfermann Verlag, Paderborn

Mohr, Bärbel (2004), Bestellungen beim Universum. Ein Handbuch zur Wunscherfüllung, 14. Auflage;
Omega-Verlag, Aachen

Murphy, Joseph (2005), Die Macht Ihres Unterbewusstseins. Affirmationen für Glück und Erfolg;
Ariston Verlag, München
Rand, Ayn (1964), The Virtue of Selfishness;
Signet, New York NY

Rizzolatti, Giacomo und Sinigaglia, Corrado (2008), Empathie und Spiegelneurone: Die biologische Basis des Mitgefühls;
Suhrkamp Verlag, Berlin

Rosen, Sidney (Hrsg.) (2006), Die Lehrgeschichten von Milton H. Erickson, 8. Auflage;
Iskopress, Salzhausen

Satir, Virginia (2004), Kommunikation, Selbstwert, Kongruenz: Konzepte und Perspektiven familientherapeutischer Praxis;
Junfermann Verlag, Paderborn

Schultz, Johannes (2010), Autogenes Training: Das Original Übungsheft: Die Anleitung vom Begründer der Selbstentspannung, 25. Auflage;
Trias Verlag, Stuttgart

Shapiro, Francine und Forrest, Margot (2007), EMDR in Aktion: Die neue Kurzzeit-Therapie in der Praxis, 3. Auflage;
Junfermann Verlag, Paderborn

Watzlawick, Paul und Beavin, Janet und Jackson, Don (2003), Menschliche Kommunikation, Formen, Störungen, Paradoxien, Nachdruck der 10. Auflage;
Verlag Hans Huber, Bern